Innovation in Law Firms: Implementing Successful Projects

STUART WHITTLE
CATRIONA WOLFENDEN

Commissioning editor
Alex Davies

Managing director
Sian O'Neill

Innovation in Law Firms: Implementing Successful Projects
is published by

Globe Law and Business Ltd
3 Mylor Close
Horsell
Woking
Surrey GU21 4DD
United Kingdom
Tel: +44 20 3745 4770
www.globelawandbusiness.com

Innovation in Law Firms: Implementing Successful Projects

ISBN 978-1-78742-955-0
EPUB ISBN 978-1-78742-956-7
Adobe PDF ISBN 978-1-78742-957-4

Contents

About the authors

Stuart Whittle – chief innovation and technology officer at Weightmans LLP

Stuart is a true legal innovator, recently described as "a living Action Man of legal innovation" by industry peers. Having qualified as a lawyer in 1995, he specialized in professional indemnity from then until he became the head of Weightmans' IT department ten years later. Stuart's interest in technology and innovation manifested itself early on in his career when, as part of the last seat of his training contract, he was assigned to work with the then IT partner. During that time, he built a database to help deal with claims relating to a major piece of litigation and also created Weightmans' first intranet.

In 2002, he was promoted to partner. From 2003 onwards, Stuart became involved in Weightmans' IT, designing, developing, and rolling out CMSs across the firm. In 2005, he took on responsibility for Weightmans' IT department and in 2010 was promoted to IS and operations director and became a member of Weightmans' Board.

Following Weightmans' strategic review in 2017, Stuart was appointed business services and innovation director with responsibility for facilities, people and knowledge, business change, information management and technology, innovation, and risk and compliance. His current role as chief technology and innovation officer dates from 2023, having been tasked to set up a new product and innovation department to systematize Weightmans' approach to developing products that help meet client needs.

Stuart regularly presents at events with special areas of interest being around business process redesign – helping lawyers to work smartly in an uncertain market where prices are being squeezed and the quality of the service that is delivered to the client needs to be continually improved.

He has a Masters in Information Technology, is a qualified coach, a Chartered IT professional, and a certified Lean Six Sigma Master Black Belt.

Stuart is a director of the Legal IT Innovators Group, a not for profit organization run by and for its members. Stuart also set up and, until 2024, chaired the MatterSphere User Group. In 2013 Stuart was named one of Legal Business' CIO Powerlist. He was nominated for the Lawyer's Business Leader of the Year in 2015 and 2016 saw *Legal Week* rank him as one of its top 20 Innovators. He won the Innovation Trailblazer Award at the Legal Innovation Awards 2022.

Dr Catriona Wolfenden – director of product and innovation at Weightmans LLP

Catriona leads innovation and product initiatives across Weightmans, ensuring that delivery is aligned to the firm's overall strategy. She works closely with the innovation and product teams, clients, suppliers, and legal teams to ensure that Weightmans continues to evolve and offer market-leading solutions.

Catriona joined Weightmans in September 2007 following completion of a PhD in medical law and the Bar Vocational Course. She was admitted as a solicitor in October 2011 and promoted to partner in 2019. Catriona has plenty of first-hand experience of civil litigation as she was a team leader in the costs department and, as a professional support lawyer, frequently provided strategic know-how updates, training, and technical support both internally and externally for clients.

Catriona is regularly interviewed for articles and research projects and frequently presents at legal and innovation conferences on topics related to innovation and future skills. She was shortlisted for "rising star" at the *Legal Week* Innovation Awards 2019. Catriona's team have been shortlisted finalists in 22 National Innovation awards since 2018, winning the Modern Law Awards 2019 for the "Best use of technology" as a result of a collaborative project with Kira Systems and the Computer Science Department at the University of Liverpool. They were runner-up at the British Legal Tech Awards 2020 for "Technology Venture of the Year" for an RPA EFA and runner-up for "Most Innovative Firm" at the British Legal Tech Awards 2022.

Catriona has been a director of the LegalTech Association for the UK (UKLTA) and completed a three-year term on the Liverpool Enterprise Partnership Professional and Business Services Board. Catriona is a member of UK Research and Innovation Future Leaders Fellowship Panel College.

Acknowledgments

Stuart

I started my Master's degree in IT in 2000 whilst working full-time as a solicitor at Weightmans. It should have been an 18-month course – each module was eight weeks long with, in theory, two weeks between the next module. I found the combination of studying and working so exhausting that I ended up having to do eight weeks on, ten weeks off. I got three months into my six-month dissertation, only to be told that my subject matter was insufficiently academic. The only reason I started again and finished my dissertation was because I knew future me would look back in five years' time and wonder why I did not just get it over the line. All in all, the degree took me four years to complete and, looking back, the baseline grounding it gave me in all things IT has been invaluable. That said, I did promise myself that I would never study and work full-time at the same time ever again.

I anticipate you can already see the parallels. I am sure the phrase "everyone has a book in them" is familiar to most but, as it turns out, I had probably a third-to-half of a book in me and I am desperately hoping that that half doesn't fulfil the other half of the phrase. In terms of the idea, inviting me to contribute and, frankly, getting this over the line, I of course have Cat to thank, not least as I was entirely prepared to abandon the venture at a number of points (despite knowing that my future self would look back in five years' time and wonder why I did not get it over the line). If there ever was someone who personified the phrase, "If you want something done, give it to a busy woman", then Cat is that person. Suffice it to say, this is the last time I write a book.

The other person to whom in large part I owe the trajectory of my career is my former boss, Frank Maher. Ultimately it was working for him and the opportunities he gave me (including pushing me to do a Master's) that inspired me to change my career path so I could try and help lawyers use technology in their legal practice of solving clients' problems. I also should thank my peers in other firms and organizations, particularly those who I have met through my involvement in Litig, who have been unfailingly generous and supportive over the years in one way or another. There are too many to mention individually who have had a hugely positive impact on my career (whether they know it or not) but I should single out Derek Southall, who I have known for nearly 20 years now and who has kindly agreed to write the foreword to this book. If there is anyone in the legal IT industry who personifies the generous and supportive attitude of the community, it is Derek.

Cat and I collectively need to thank Globe Law and Business for their patience in our repeated failure to hit any deadline, which reminded me of the Douglas Adams quote: "I love deadlines; I like the whooshing sound they make as they fly by". We are both appreciative of the opportunities our time at Weightmans has afforded us to try new things and to have a career that is very far removed from the ones we thought we would have!

Catriona

I was finishing off my PhD when I met my now husband and he volunteered to read it all. It was a heavy read and he suggested something a bit lighter if I ever wrote anything substantial again; hopefully, this fits the bill. I am very grateful to Peter for his unwavering support in everything I do, and for not batting an eyelid when I said I was going to write a book, despite knowing the time it would take for me to be able to do it. Thanks also to Freddie, who commented, "It must be hard to write a book, Mum, but if you get short on words just fill some pages with THE END on repeat". Thanks also to my parents and siblings (and wider family) for their support and laughs along the way.

I moved into innovation having practiced as a lawyer and then via a knowledge management route. I had absolutely no idea what I was doing, but I knew it was an opportunity I had to take. Stu talks of Frank giving him the opportunity to change the trajectory of his career; Stu has done the same for me, for which I am very grateful. Stu has given me countless opportunities to enhance my skill set (sometimes despite my protestations!), and a confidence push when required so I have had fleeting moments when I think I can do this, as well as enough constructive challenge to be able to see other ways of solving the same problem. Rob Williams started the innovation "journey" with us, seeing the possibility early on, and continues to be a supportive sounding board and a much-appreciated mentor. I may be biased, but I am pretty sure I have the best product and innovation colleagues to work with – we have had many laughs and late nights along the way working out how the heck we could get product and innovation to work in a law firm. Thanks for your boundless enthusiasm and bravery.

Disclaimer

You cannot take the lawyer out of us! We have taken a light-hearted and somewhat tongue-in-cheek approach when writing this book, with a view to making some serious points around innovation in law firms. The contents of this book are an amalgamation of our hard-won experience over many years, including conversations with the wider legal innovation community to create pastiches of experiences that we and others in that community have experienced whilst working in innovation in law firms of various sizes, or from vendors and others who attempt to work with us.

Introduction: What has *Donoghue v. Stevenson* got to do with innovation?

On 26 August 1928, a shop assistant was bought a bottle of ginger beer by her friend in a café in Paisley. The bottle was made from dark opaque glass and some of the drink was poured into a tumbler and drunk by the shop assistant. As her friend poured the remainder of the drink into the tumbler, a decomposed snail fell out of the bottle. The snail could not have been detected until the majority of the bottle had been consumed. The shop assistant became ill, both at the shock of the sight of the snail and with gastroenteritis from the drink she had consumed before being aware of the snail. The shop assistant brought a claim against the manufacturer who had bottled and labelled the drink, for her injuries. She claimed that the manufacturer had a duty to ensure a system of working that would prevent snails getting into the bottle and a system to inspect the bottle before filling them and had failed on both accounts. The shop assistant was Mrs Donoghue. When she drank the ginger beer nearly 100 years ago, she could not have anticipated that her case[1] would be so seminal that every law student since can quote it and knows that it established the principle of the duty of care in tort with Lord Atkin's famous neighbor dictum,[2] which has spawned many subsequent landmark cases. If that is not lawyers being innovative, then we do not know what is. The trouble is, lawyers do not see themselves as innovative – but researching the law, producing novel arguments, and challenging case law and legislation are all skills that demonstrate innovation.

It is important in the context of innovation to realize that lawyers have always innovated. Lawyers' core competency is the law, it is what they do. They innovate in their core competency all the time. They advise clients how to conduct business legally within a complex regulatory environment; they advise clients on the most tax-efficient deal structures; and they continually test the boundaries of the law by taking novel points based on innovative legal argument to the highest courts of the land. We have seen the rise of ChatGPT and other large language models (LLMs) as we have been writing this book and seen articles arguing about the position in relation to copyright and how it can be applied to LLMs – all novel and innovative applications of the law to a new factual matrix.[3]

So, why do law firms and lawyers struggle with innovation? Arguments from lawyers typically center around a couple of core strands that may exist in combination and include "It isn't my job", "I don't have the time", "I am not a coder", or "They are my clients". However, lawyers often recognize that they need *something* innovative, even if they do not know what that something looks like!

So, whose job is it? You may be reading this because you have innovation in your job title and work in a professional services firm. You may be a student wanting to know more about how innovation works in a law firm, or you may be a lawyer wondering the same thing! You may be wondering about a move into lawtech, either in a professional services firm or a solutions provider. You may be in-house, wondering what you can ask your law firm to do or what you can recycle to make your own department more innovative. You may be a consumer of legal services, wondering what all of this means to you. You may not fall into any of these categories – you do not need innovation in your job title to be innovative and try new things. As the saying goes, *"If you always do what you always did, you will always get what you always got"*.

Clients are the main driver for innovation in a law firm as they ask us to innovate. They are not always sure what they mean, but generally it boils down to:

- Seeking better value for money when they have less to spend on legal fees;
- Hoping that you might understand and solve their problems; and
- Improving the impression they can present to their boss by returning with added value.

As a lawyer, it may not feel like this drive for innovation is affecting you at 3pm on a Wednesday afternoon when you are head down in your files as yesterday was very much like today in that respect. However, as you become more senior in a law firm, part of your role is to think about the business more widely and anticipate what is coming down the line for your clients, their sectors, and their markets. Despite the fact that it probably feels like nothing much changes, until it does. By which time, it is often too late.[4]

The COVID-19 pandemic has accelerated our industry's reliance on technology and our ability to work entirely digitally by about five to ten years (depending on who you believe). Having had home working forced upon us by necessity during that time, perhaps to our surprise, it worked. Mostly. What happened to us and what happened to our clients was the same. Pre-pandemic, the prevailing (entirely incorrect) opinion was that it was simply impossible to work remotely and digitally for any length of time. If lawyers were prepared to grudgingly admit that it was not, technically, impossible, it was at least entirely impractical. A view that entirely changed overnight. Not only did it work, some people actually preferred to work digitally and many law firms have remained hybrid, with varying degrees of time working in the office and from other (often home-based) locations. This digital acceleration applies to our clients too and we have seen a steady increase in clients who historically may not have been interested in innovation and digital transformation who have now started to embrace it.

1 *Donoghue (Pauper) v. Stevenson* (1932) A.C 562.

2 "The rule that you are to love your neighbour becomes in law, you must not injure your neighbour; and the lawyer's question, Who is my neighbour? receives a restricted reply. You must take reasonable care to avoid acts or omissions which you can reasonably foresee would be likely to injure your neighbour. Who, then, in law is my neighbour? The answer seems to be – persons who are so closely and directly affected by my act that I ought reasonably to have them in contemplation as being so affected when I am directing my mind to the acts or omissions which are called in question." *Donoghue (Pauper) v. Stevenson* (1932) A.C 562, 580 (Atkin LJ).

3 Jodha, D., and Bera, P., "Copyright Issues in the Era of AI – A Critical Analysis", *Res Militaris: Social Science Journal*, Volume 13, issue 3, 2023. See: https://resmilitaris.net/issue-content/copyright-issues-in-the-era-of-ai-a-critical-analysis-2247; Botev, V., "How can developers train AI models without violating copyright?", 30 April 2023. See: https://tech.eu/2023/04/30/how-can-developers-train-ai-models-without-violating-copyright/; Willinsky, J., "The Intellectual Property Rights and Existential Threat of Large Language Models", May 2023. See: www.slaw.ca/2023/05/11/the-intellectual-property-rights-and-existential-threat-of-large-language-models/; Porsdam Mann, S., Earp, B., Nyholm, S., et al. "Generative AI entails a credit–blame asymmetry", *Nat Mach Intell* 5, 472–475, May 2023. See: https://doi.org/10.1038/s42256-023-00653-1.

4 Snook, S., "Each uneventful day that passes reinforces the steadily growing false sense of confidence that everything is alright. That I, we, my group, must be OK, because the way we did things today resulted in no adverse consequences." Associate Professor of Organization Behavior at the Harvard Business School.

Chapter 1: A faster horse or the moon on a stick?

We have worked in the legal industry for a combined total of 46 years. When Stuart started work in 1993, insofar as the legal industry was concerned, for the most part the fledgling internet and world wide web may as well have not existed. The firm he joined had analogue telephones, a fax, the slightly mysterious telex, and the splendidly named Wang – a green screen word processing system. Everything was managed with paper – paper files, paper books, research, paper invoices, paper diaries, paper documents, paper plans, paper memos with everything duplicated using carbon copy paper.[1] We handwrote amendments on pleadings (or stapled strips of paper if there was no room for the amendment) using a specified order of ink colors (red, green, violet, yellow) for each subsequent amendment. Updates to court reports and reference books were physically glued into the books by the librarians, pending the next edition. Travelling drafts of documents were amended by hand, again in different colors for each amendment stage, and using a convoluted system of asterisks and superscript characters to reference amendments written on other pages or supplemental pages. Then the final clean draft would need to be read through by two trainees, side by side, to make sure the clean draft captured all of the agreed handwritten amendments. In many ways, the lawyers who lived and practiced law during this period look back with fondness at a world and a way of working that was, at a fundamental level, simpler.

Despite the rise in technology, for the majority of the past 30 years, at a very basic level, lawyers have continued to do the same ten or so things with some, frankly, minor incremental rather than fundamental, changes enabled by computers. Namely, lawyers:

- Draft letters and, these days, emails, which perform the same function;
- Draft documents including leases, contracts, pleadings, and witness statements;
- Review and amend those documents by emailing them back and forth;
- Make telephone calls (although much less these days than we used to – there seems to be a generational abhorrence at the suggestion you

might pick up the telephone to talk to another human being, especially one you have never met before);
- Attend meetings (with the client, the other side, witnesses, experts and so on);
- Attend courts, tribunals, mediations, arbitrations and so on;
- Draft notes (of telephone calls, meetings, hearings and so on – well, that's what best practice suggests they do at the very least);
- Dictate (and more often these days, actually type);
- Record time;
- Bill (and chase for payment); and
- Undertake legal research (but only if you cannot find a trainee to do it for you and are really desperate).

We would argue that the way in which technology has changed how these activities are now done, is, for a lot of lawyers, a mixed blessing. Email is an instantaneous, superficially efficient means of exchanging information but it has come with a society-wide, increased expectation for an immediate response with commensurately less time for a lawyer to give time and thought to a more considered and nuanced one. Likewise, the ease of production of an email has simply led to a proliferation of them, with the universally hated back-covering cc'ings and bcc'ings. Similar to the invention of the washing machine; the fact that it made washing clothes less of a chore simply led to clothes being washed more frequently with no overall time saving.[2] Gone are the days of receiving a letter, letting it percolate about in the back of your subconscious before dictating a response and then waiting a few days to get the dictated version back, allowing for another couple of days of percolation to refine the original thoughts, amend the dictated letter before finally putting it in the post, safe in the knowledge it would be a month before you get a response. The ease with which emails can be generated and sent off has led to a volume of emails that lawyers, and indeed their clients, can find truly overwhelming.

In a similar way, when undertaking legal research, free text searching is an incredibly powerful tool for legal research when coupled with Boolean operators. But in the absence of sophisticated searching techniques on the part of individual lawyers (we don't know many who are fluent users of Boolean operators), it typically massively increases the volume of potential sources for the lawyer to review and the concomitant fear on the part of the lawyer that they might have missed something. The ease with which information and documentation can be created, replicated, and disseminated has changed the disclosure landscape for litigation beyond comprehension, such that we have had to invent electronic solutions (for example, eDisclosure systems) to help deal with the volume of documents that require reviewing. This is before we even contemplate what generative AI may do for the legal industry, which will no doubt be the subject for many future books. That said, whatever large language models (LLMs) ultimately end up doing, we are confident that as the cost and effort involved in producing content reduces, so there will simply be more content created and generative AI may end up eating itself as it trains itself on content that it wrote.[3]

It has always been a challenge as a practicing lawyer to do the day job and keep up to date with the law. Now, not only do you have perform the day job, ensuring that what you are doing is compliant with the latest regulatory legislation and internal and external standards, you also have to learn to use the many and disparate software applications that your catastrophically helpful IT teams have provided for you.

Of Stuart's 30 years in the legal industry, 20 have been involved in the legal IT community. At the start of his involvement in legal technology, there were a number of firms doing many different things with a lot of different vendors supplying software of varying efficacy. Over the years, most firms have broadly ended up with a very similar suite of application-based functionality, namely practice management systems, document management systems, case management systems, workflow systems, client-relationship management (CRM) systems, HR systems, reporting systems, and digital dictation systems. The majority of this technology is aimed at improving the efficiencies of the business of doing law (or at least it is sold on this basis); whether it does is, at best, a moot point, as often too much time is spent dealing with the software itself rather than examining and standardizing the tasks that technology is designed to support. This is glibly equated with efficiency on the basis that technology could perform repeatable and predictable tasks at scale. Which of course it can, but only if the technology is used in the process, and there is a question over how much efficiency is actually gained.[4] A lot of the technology in law firms is intended to help with the repeatable and predictable elements of the way that lawyers work by reducing the need to reinvent the wheel, help with regulatory and compliance hoops, and to automate repeatable and predictable tasks. However brilliant and "*intuitive*" the technology is, for it to be effective it requires lawyers to work in a repeatable and predictable way. At one level, if they are not working in the way that the technology was anticipating, then the technology does not help them as it cannot be designed around each lawyer's unique way of working. Where law firms do not deal with standardization and the concomitant change management, throwing technology at people and process issues simply results in faster and more efficient chaos. At best we suspect, a bit like eDisclosure, the technologies are simply responses to help manage increasing complexity (and in the process adding additional layers of complexity from the perspective of lawyers). This has led to today's situation in which the people element of change management has been overlooked, which in turn has created the somewhat chaotic environment in which many of us are trying to innovate.

Inevitably, with a fragmented and disparate market there then came a period of consolidation that reduced the choice available without necessarily improving the offering from the point of view of the lawyers. So, we ended up with most firms having one of something from a limited number of vendors and from the point of view of a technologist, frankly, it all got a bit dull. The best that law firm IT departments were able to deliver internally was application-based computing. The applications created or suggested by the IT department were not always intuitive, memorable, or used regularly enough to become familiar to the lawyers, It is little wonder that most then stuck to Outlook and Word.

What you should be noticing in this necessarily high-level perspective is that there was never very much discussion about the client in all of this. It was all about the law firms' lawyers. There were some sectors where use of the technology was becoming more client-facing, but they tended to be the exception rather than rule. Why, if you were a big organization, would you really be going to a law firm to deliver a technology solution?

Then, circa 2016, seemingly out of the blue, a number of interesting-looking solutions appeared from a remarkable number of small start-ups that had had been toiling away in the background for a number of years, seemingly gaining little traction.[5] At the same time, corporate, public sector, and third sector clients started asking law firms to showcase how they were using technology to help deliver their legal services more efficiently and to elucidate their approach to innovation, which leads neatly on to the next section.

Client-led innovation[6]

The legal industry is highly competitive. It is a daily challenge to ensure that you are delivering value from the perspective of your clients (with every client defining that value differently – even clients in the same sector, doing the same sort of business) so that they continue to be happy to instruct you, to help existing clients with additional solutions, and to deliver solutions to new clients. Additionally, law firms are driven by the needs of their clients and have to continue to adapt as the legislative and regulatory environment develops, as the market changes, and as the needs of their clients change over time. Clients' consistent refrain is that their legal spend is too high and that their lawyers do not understand their business, but nevertheless they have a choice as to where they put their (too high) spend and which lawyers (who don't understand their business) they instruct. As a result, change in law firms (over and above regulatory and legislative requirements) is more often than not driven by clients, certainly from the perspective of a law firm if not from the perspective of the clients.

The pressures clients face that lead to innovation

In a law firm, the firm revolves around the lawyers. The business services functions, especially the IT function, revolve around the lawyers. That's not a surprise; that's the core business of the law firm – doing the law and everything else within the firm is set up to support that. The situation is very different for in-house counsel as law is not the core business of the organization, be it a commercial one, a public body, or a charity. The support functions are built around the core competencies of the organization, whatever that may be, and the in-house legal team is simply another of those support functions. There are a number of consequences of this for an in-house legal team. Firstly, as a "*support*" function they are now part of the cost base and no longer can they say to IT, HR, or Marketing, "*Don't you know, I pay your wages?*" (Yes, anecdotally, that still happens). The business is now saying that to them. Secondly, the world has stopped revolving around them and their needs and, in particular, a lot of the IT systems and support they might have had access to in private practice simply does not exist and, even more, when they do ask for time from the organization's IT team, they are quite a long way down the list of priorities that that finite resource has. Over time, as business activity increases, so does the legal activity required of in-house teams and potential litigation, whether it be dealing with higher volumes of contracts, higher volumes of increasingly complex litigation (and potential litigation), or increasingly complex regulatory environments to navigate. However, the 2021 EY survey report[7] states that 88 percent of general counsel expect legal spend to reduce, necessarily leading to workloads exceeding budgets and capacity.

So, as a support function to a larger organization, they are asked about the innovation they can bring to, for example, improve the bottom line. They are also charged with controlling their department's cost, which, over and above head count, will largely be their spend with private practice law firms (and increasingly, alternative legal service providers (ALSPs)). Most in-house teams will tell you that their remit has exponentially expanded, as has the complexity of the organizations for whom they work and the relevant regulatory and legislative environment – all without a commensurate increase in budget or resource.

Like most lawyers, we do not recall the "innovation" option at university or law college and so when in-house counsel are challenged by their organizations around how they are innovating, it can be a real struggle. Increased demand, cost, and resource constraints – and the business is asking them to be innovative too. However, help is at hand for in-house counsel. For those large organizations who have an element of buying power, there are a lot of law firms who would like their business (see above about the competitive environment). The organizations pay these law firms a lot of money (from the organization's perspective) and these law firms seem to have deep pockets (with net margins most commercial organizations would die for). Taking all of that in the round, this means that in-house law teams have (in the last four or five years) turned to their law firms asking them for examples (that they can take back into their organizations) of things that look like innovation, technology, and efficiencies so they can demonstrate that they are adding value and, to boot, doing more for less.

Driven by the changing needs of clients, law firms have been looking to see how they can meet those needs. At a very basic level, this has included delivering services differently, developing new services to address existing and new problems, and trying to use technology to solve problems that are repeatable and predictable and require scale beyond throwing (expensive) people at the problem. Alongside this is the proliferation of modules at university on lawtech,[8] the increasingly popularity of the "O shaped lawyer"[9] and books such as Adam Curphey's excellent *The Legal Team of the Future: Law+ Skills*.[10]

The client focus of law – outcomes, not hours with lawyers

As Susskind and Susskind have said, and we paraphrase, it does not matter how lovely we think we are as lawyers, our clients do not really want to spend time with us. They want the outcome achieved and we lawyers are a necessary evil and, even in a lot of cases, a distress purchase necessary to achieving the clients' outcome.[11] They want to sell their company, they want to navigate a regulatory landscape ethically and legally, they want their case settled. They have a problem and they want us to make it go away. If they could have solved the problem themselves, they would have done so already. They do not want our treatise on competition law and how it applies to their issue. They only want to know what actual, practical steps they need to take to achieve their outcome within the bounds of the law and, for the in-house team that are organizationally on the hook for instructing you, it would be really nice if you could make them look good in the process (in particular, do not cause them problems by equivocating, changing your advice at the last minute, surprising them with a bill the size of which they were not expecting and so on). The individuals who are instructing you as a lawyer have their own bosses, their own challenges, their own objectives. In terms of what it takes to make your clients look good, understanding the drivers for the individual at the company is key. As a general rule, over the last four or five years, this has included innovation and technology-led solutions that in-house teams can take to the wider business to help them justify their existence and become seen not just as a cost base, but rather an integral part of helping drive the organization's goals.

Competition and fear of missing out

With this increased focus on technology, innovation, and efficiencies, law firms gradually started to invest in teams of people to help them answer the questions that clients were asking them. For a lot of firms, the natural home for some of this work lay with the knowledge management teams who understood the law, were increasingly engaging with clients directly, and, dare we argue, did not have the pressure of chargeable hours and revenue targets. That is not to say that firms did not hire people from outside of the industry, but some of the most interesting things that were happening early doors impressionistically emanated from the firms' knowledge management teams. Innovation is hard. Technology development, implementation, and adoption is hard. Innovation coupled with technology implementation is hard squared. Which means it all takes time, and it always takes longer than you first think. Whilst the knowledge management teams were not idle before, they did have the freedom to refocus their time free from revenue and hours targets. This is what Catriona did. Originally part of our knowledge management team, in the early days of our journey we refocused her time away from knowledge management and into innovation.

In an effort to gain further value from explosive innovation within firms and to help create a positive impression with clients, there was also a lot of innovation by PR. That in turn drove more innovation by PR with law firms competing to create the most favorable impression. We all played the game. The hype around AI had grown to such a level that in 2019 it was reported that 40 percent of 'AI start-ups' in Europe did not actually use AI.[12] A testament to how the market has changed is that around the same time as this we saw the first categories related to the "Best innovation in..." in a lot of the markets' awards recognition competitions, in the same way that we are seeing a lot of the "Best ESG in..." for environmental, social, and governance (ESG) in 2024.

All of this became self-perpetuating in that partners in law firms looked at other law firms' PR and awards and would turn inwards and ask of their firm, *"Look at all this, what are we doing about innovation?"* when struggling to have anything substantive to put into responses to invitations to tender (ITTs) where they were being asked about innovations, technologies, and efficiencies. That fear of missing out, the increased competition, and the increased focus of clients on innovation, all drove the rise of innovation teams within law firms. The reader may see analogies in all of this with the current response to Generative AI, but we leave that for history to sort out.

Solving business problems, not just legal ones – the holistic advisor

Whether this is deliberate on the part of the in-house teams or an accidental consequence, asking the question around what innovation and technology the law firm can bring to the relationship exposes how well the law firm truly understands the clients' organization, and which of their challenges are ones that law firms can address. Generic responses detailing law firms' capabilities are meaningless unless the law firm can link it with a problem that the organization has and explain how the law firm's capability in that area actually helps the client; the, *"So what?"* question. Trite though it is, you need to explain what is in it for the client. Many law firms have the experience of developing solutions for a particular client in a particular sector, which thinks it is the best thing since sliced bread only to be dismayed that the same sort of client in the same sector looks at the thing and responds unenthusiastically. The point is that law firms cannot innovate in a vacuum. They need to properly understand what is the actual problem that the client needs solving and then explore with the client what sort of price they might be prepared to pay, should the law firms identify solutions. There is no point having the best idea in the world if no one wants to buy it from you or if you make a loss selling it.

The business of law

Thirty years ago, the business model of a law firm was relatively straightforward and it was quite difficult to run a law firm so badly that it failed. The regulatory environment was, essentially, non-existent (or at best, pretty benign) compared to today when you take into account requirements around money laundering, knowing your client, anti-bribery, anti-slavery, data protection, and information security more generally. Overheads were pretty constrained, the main cost after salaries was premises, and the rule of thumb was that you split revenue into three – a third for salaries, a third for overheads, and a third for the partners. Post-qualification lockstep, in which every year you aged resulted in an increase in your salary (because you were more experienced) essentially, paid for itself as clients could be charged a higher hourly rate for more experienced lawyers. Work came in and marketing consisted of taking clients for a decent meal and paying for some boozy nights out or a round of golf or hospitality at a major sporting event. Preferably all four. In short succession. The most difficult conversation you had to have with a client was at the beginning of each financial year, explaining to them that you were having to increase your hourly rates by ten percent across the board. It was a profession far more than a business and, as a profession, it considered that clients should count themselves lucky to be the beneficiaries of its considered advice. We accept this is a caricature but, like all good caricatures, it holds an essence of truth.

An evolving profession with new challenges

All of this started to change as law firms grew and clients started to realize that they held the buying power, coupled with the rise of procurement professionals who started to turn their eyes to their organizations' legal spends. At a basic level, for anything short of a *"bet-the-company"* type of concern, there were a lot of lawyers, doing, for the most part, very similar things in very similar ways. For the first time, law firms were being asked to respond to tenders and clients were starting to ask difficult questions, prompted by how procurement professionals dealt with their organizations' wider supply chain, around, in effect, discounts and added value in return for the volume of work that the client was generating for the firm. Law firms responded as they had to in order to continue to work for their clients.

The rise of the "nons" and learning from other industries

As firms grew, they started to find that in order to manage the growing business they needed to put in place policies and procedures. These all needed more managing than the partners responsible for these areas of the business had the time to do in addition to their day job of advising clients and generating revenue and winning business. As a result, you started to see the rise of the "nons" in law firms (often used in a derogatory sense by the lawyers) – the non-lawyers,[13] the "cost centers". Law firms started to hire professionals from other organizations to run their HR, marketing, and IT functions, with those heading up those departments reporting to the managing partner whose role started to morph into, effectively, COO. The definition of these professionals by what they were not (i.e. not lawyers) was (and still is, to an extent) a real reflection of lawyers' ontology of the world in which they divided the world neatly in two; "lawyers" and "everyone else", with the assumption that everyone in the "everyone else" category had joined a law firm because at some point they would want to "progress" and become lawyers.[14] The "nons" had a really hard time in law firms in the early days where every decision would be second-guessed by one or more partners who assumed that their intelligence meant they were perfectly entitled to dictate what needed to be done, regardless of the fact that they had no relevant qualifications nor 20 years' experience in HR or Marketing or IT; however, it was the start of the "professionalization" of law firm management. By definition, most of these people had not worked for law firms before and brought insight and practices from other industries, and slowly you started to see these insights influence how law firms were being managed.

The changing business model for legal service

Law firms continued to expand. Clients' procurement teams became more sophisticated when procuring legal services. Clients were starting to ask how firms were assuring quality, and efficient and consistent service, how law firms were managed, and how law firms were using technology. The regulatory environment continued to change. Attitudes to information security evolved from the single question, "Do you have an IT security policy?"' into questionnaires about information and cyber security running to hundreds of questions in length. All these drivers affected the running of law firms, generating the need for those firms to create specialist business services functions within the firms to enable all of this to be managed. Over time, heads of HR, marketing, and IT morphed into HR directors, marketing directors, IT directors and, more recently, into chief personnel officers, chief marketing officers, and chief technology officers as law firms mirrored what they were seeing in their larger corporate clients.

The rise of the innovation team

Many factors contributed to the rise of the innovation team:

- An evolving technology landscape.
- Clients making more and more use of their buying power.
- In-house teams coming under pressure to be "innovative" and improve efficiencies using technology (synonyms for saving cost).
- The vast amounts of innovation by PR in the legal press.
- Increasing demands from law firm partners to their Boards to "do something about innovation".

Interestingly, ten to 15 years earlier, law firms looked specifically to their IT teams to deliver innovations. Indeed, 20 years ago, a non-profit organization run by its members, for its members, was created and titled The Legal IT Innovation Group to reflect the innovation brought into law firms by their IT teams. In the early 2000s there were a lot of interesting activities from law firms' IT teams, albeit not specifically under the banner of "innovation" so much as technology, and law firms' IT teams won awards for the work they were doing, which at the time included a lot of client-facing technology.

However, the genesis of actual innovation teams tended not to come from the IT teams as much as the knowledge management teams. This may be regarded as slightly surprising as, for a lot of the time, innovation was synonymous with technology. We think that the reasons for this are multi-faceted. Firstly, over time, the complexity of law firms' information technology estate increased and, with that, came an increasing complexity in managing business as usual. Law firms became less tolerant of any system down time. The majority of the law firms' IT team's time was spent on managing this complexity. On top of that complexity, increasing demands to continually improve the firms' information security and comply with standards such as ISO 27001 and Cyber Essentials Plus added to management overheads and meant that law firms' IT departments became less and less directly exposed to clients. In contrast to that, the market started to see firms' knowledge management teams engaging more directly with clients and providing services to them as well as to the law firms' own lawyers. Knowledge management teams that were, perhaps, less constrained by chargeable hours targets, had a bit more time to experiment with technology and were thus able to think a bit more about how technology might support the needs of the clients. They had also seen the portals brought into some areas of law, such as personal injury, and would often help on client projects – such as bulk document review. A final factor was that almost all of the technology solutions from start-ups were cloud first, which meant that the knowledge management teams that were looking at the technology needed far less time from their IT departments to get up and running and to simply experiment.

"In a law firm, if it isn't somebody's job, it doesn't get done."[15] Over time, the individuals who were dabbling in innovation, in the loosest sense of the word, were tasked with converting that dabbling into a team that could deliver solutions to clients and to their own lawyers. The roles in those teams were largely new to the industry if not completely invented and so we all came up with some interesting job titles – the most common of which were legal engineer or legal technologist (there were other, more creative, job titles like "legal tech evangelist" and "change maker"). The people recruited into these roles tended to be younger lawyers with an enthusiasm for technology who had had enough of the chargeable hours rat race. Thus were born firms' innovation teams, or at least that was how we did it! There are contrasting views as to whether that was universally the right thing to do – by way of analogy, if you were running a technology firm and needed an in-house legal function, it would seem unlikely that you would ask one of your developers to take on that role...

References

1 Carbon copy paper created simultaneous copies of a document when written on with ball point pen, or back in the day, used with a typewriter.

2 Harford, T., *Fifty Things that Made the Modern Economy*, London: Little Brown, 2017: "The washing machine didn't save a lot of time because we didn't wash clothes very often...The washing machine didn't save much time, and the ready meal did, because we were willing to stink but we weren't willing to starve."

3 Wong, M., "AI is an Existential Threat to Itself", 21 June 2023. See: www.theatlantic.com/technology/archive/2023/06/generative-ai-future-training-models/674478/.

4 There is a long-running discussion about whether efficiency is even desired by law firms, but that is not addressed in this book.

5 This included the first British Legal Technology Forum in 2015, the first Legal Geek Conference (for LegalTech start-ups) in 2016 – www.legalgeek.co/about-us/, the first British Legal Technology Awards in 2017, and Future Lawyer Week in 2017.

6 By client, we usually mean institutional clients rather than acting for private individuals.

7 Grossman, C., "The General Counsel Imperative: How do you turn barriers into building blocks?" 7 April 2021. See: www.ey.com/en_gr/law/general-counsel-imperative-barriers-building-blocks.

8 For example, www.law.ac.uk/study/postgraduate/law/msc-legal-technology/

9 https://oshaped.com/the-o-shaped-mindset-and-attributes

10 Curphey, A., *The Legal Team of the Future: Law+ Skills*, London: London Publishing Partnership, 2022.

11 Susskind, R. and Susskind, D., *The Future of the Professions: How Technology will Transform the Work of Human Experts*, Oxford: Oxford University Press, 2016: "Time-based billing is most likely to be displaced across the professions [...] on the basis of the value of the performance or outcome delivered."; Susskind, R., *Tomorrow's Lawyers: An Introduction to Your Future*, Oxford: Oxford University Press, 2017: "All too often, the number of hours spent by a law firm bears little relation to the value that is bought" ; Susskind, R., *The End of Lawyers?: Rethinking the Nature of Legal Services*, Oxford: Oxford University Press, 2008: "So long as the focal point of law firms' profitability is premised on the number of hours spent advising clients, their motivation will always tend to be to spend more rather than less time on their work, where clients will prefer precisely to the contrary."

12 Vincent, J. "Forty percent of 'AI start-ups' in Europe don't actually use AI, claims report", *The Verge*, 5 March 2019. See: www.theverge.com/2019/3/5/18251326/ai-startups-europe-fake-40-percent-mmc-report. "According to the survey from London venture capital firm MMC, 40 percent of European startups that are classified as AI companies don't actually use artificial intelligence in a way that is 'material' to their businesses. MMC studied some 2,830 AI start-ups in 13 EU countries to come to its conclusion, reviewing the 'activities, focus, and funding' of each firm. 'In 40 percent of cases we could find no mention of evidence of AI,' [then] MMC Head of Research David Kelnar, who compiled the report, told Forbes. Kelnar says that this means 'companies that people assume and think are AI companies are probably not'."

13 Morse, H., "The use of 'non-lawyer' is destructive to the business of law", The Legal Watercooler, 27 August 2017. See: www.legalwatercoolerblog.com/2017/08/27/the-use-of-non-lawyer-is-destructive-to-the-business-of-law/.

14 An embarrassing admission for one of your authors, a former lawyer, was that when he moved over to the dark side of business services he was genuinely surprised to learn there were professionals with the businesses services functions with actual degrees and actual postgraduate professional qualifications in their areas of expertise who were working for law firms to help the firms in those areas in which

they had the qualifications (and more to the point 20 years of experience in those areas that lawyers did not have). In addition, these people had not joined law firms because they eventually wanted to become lawyers either. Who knew?

15 Neil Cameron from Cameron Consulting Ltd said this directly to the authors.

Chapter 2:
Getting started – big picture

Getting started with no money and no team

This is how we started. There was a growing impetus from the firm – in particular our partners, who were in turn driven by their clients, that "We need to do something about innovation" in order to respond to the changing needs and demands of our clients (particularly the sorts of things that clients were asking of their law firms in tenders). What began as general statements to anyone who would listen, that, "We must do something about innovation", then picked up on the innovation by PR that was rife at the time and morphed so that the question became aimed at the Board – "What are you, the Board, doing about innovation?". For the Board, this turned into, "What are you, Stu, doing about innovation?", innovation being synonymous with technology as "you have responsibility for technology".

So, partway through our financial year, with no budget and no team, we needed to get some people together and prove that we could do something, deliver something, achieve some successes in order to be able to put a business case together for the following year to do it properly, with a team and a budget. This became, "Cat, you are in knowledge management and seem interested in this, what can you do (for free, with no people, no experience and quickly)?". We borrowed time from a number of people around the business who were keen, hardworking, and wanted the opportunity to have a go at something different. We set about finding what we could do quickly and cheaply (ideally for free) to show what a minimum viable innovation team might look like and achieve. We put an internal chatbot together using Microsoft's QnA Maker (free); we sought (and got) funding from Innovate UK to work with SMEs and universities to fund the exploration of some ideas (NLP based redaction tools and predictive reserving – a solution in which we continued to invest once the funding ran out and indeed continue to develop to this day);[1] we worked with universities and published papers;[2] we jumped headlong into the ocean of innovation by PR, entering awards, and writing about the possibilities. It was all a bit *Cat in the Hat* (with acknowledgements to Dr Seuss), deliberately really. We were trying to create a bit of chaos, trying out a number of random approaches in the hope we might hit upon something.

We figured that we would worry about tidying it all up later[3] on the assumption we could persuade the firm that what we had achieved, on borrowed time, with no budget, was sufficient to justify the firm investing in a proper team. We also wanted to give ourselves enough experience to help us build the business case.

All of us on the team were, rightly or wrongly, making it up as we went along – which for many of us was quite an uncomfortable place to be. The transition from an existing, pre-defined role where you pretty much knew what your job entailed on a day-to-day basis, to a role that, in essence, started with a blank sheet of paper with no one telling you what they needed you to do today was a massive adjustment for some. There was no process to follow, a lot of politics to navigate, and outcomes that were often invisible early on, belying the amount of effort involved. For some, ultimately, it wasn't for them. It may have sounded like a welcome break from the nine to five, something different, perhaps something a bit easier than the day job, dare we say, but it was anything but. If anything, it required longer hours and harder work than the roles that they had come from – but for those that embraced it, they thrived and developed.

So where did our ideas come from? How did we identify the nature of the problems we were trying to solve? What were the ingredients that helped us get our innovation off the ground? What enabled us to work out how we might go about solving the problems we had identified? Firstly, it was a result of putting together a multi-disciplinary team.[4] A number of the team were lawyers (or former lawyers) from different backgrounds with different experiences, from running IT to knowledge management, some were developers, and some had business analysis and project management backgrounds. The ideas came from networking events, hearing clients speak, and engaging with those clients who were willing. We had examples of pure serendipity – one of the small to medium enterprises were referred to us because someone in the business knew them. However, everything we attempted started from the question: "What is the problem we are trying to solve?", a phrase so embedded in the culture of Weightmans that it has become its own cliché. In addition to clients and small to medium enterprises, we also engaged with software providers as there were (and still are) hundreds of legal technology start-ups.[5]

We did have to kiss a lot of frogs; we saw a lot of solutions wandering around looking for problems to solve and solutions built around a single lawyer's frustrations. However, we came across a few solutions that we added to our armory as we could see that they would have some application in our business or those of our clients. We knew that we would need senior supporters to help accelerate our efforts, and we quickly identified a handful of senior colleagues who were sympathetic and included them in our discussions and planning, especially around looking at problems faced by their clients.

Through all of this, our worry was that it would all become "someone else's job". Innovation becoming something done by those people over there (without me needing to get involved as it's "their job") and when we need a bit of innovation to impress clients, we will ask them what they have they done for us. In turn, we will act surprised when, having previously failed to engage, there are no rabbits to pull out of hats. We will talk about this in later chapters.

The importance of a vision (and Board support)

Our experimentation and somewhat, albeit deliberately, unfocused attempt helped us start to craft the vision that supported the business case. George R. R. Martin, author of the *Game of Thrones* series, describes authors as either being architects or gardeners:

> *"I think there are two types of writers, the architects and the gardeners. The architects plan everything ahead of time, like an architect building a house. They know how many rooms are going to be in the house, what kind of roof they're going to have, where the wires are going to run, what kind of plumbing there's going to be. They have the whole thing designed and blueprinted out before they even nail the first board up. The gardeners dig a hole, drop in a seed and water it. They kind of know what seed it is, they know if planted a fantasy seed or mystery seed or whatever. But as the plant comes up and they water it, they don't know how many branches it's going to have, they find out as it grows."*[6]

In the early stages, we were very much in the role of gardener – we planted a lot of seeds to see what might grow and used that experience to inform our business case. There were a number of key points we built into the business case (the vision).

Our first point that we committed to very early on was that we were never going to innovate in a vacuum. We were not intending to create a new paradigm for the delivery of legal services. We were not going to invent the legal equivalent of the iPhone or try to invent the automobile at a time when if you asked people what they wanted they would have said faster horses.[7] Instead, we were going to innovate in a context, namely to start from the position of being very clear what the problem was we were trying to solve. Whether an internal problem or a client's problem, fundamentally that was to be our starting place.

What does success look like?

In reality, a lot of innovation in law firms is not about creating something entirely new, but being able to apply existing capabilities in more imaginative ways to solve similar classes of problems in different domains. When you are starting out as an innovation team, your firm will have a set of (in our experience, under-used and under-exploited) capabilities, particularly on the technology front. As an example, a capability to record metadata for high volumes of related matters for a client, coupled with a data visualization capability to drive actionable insight applies to defendant personal injury claims, debt recovery claims, employment claims, plot sales, lease renewals, license renewals, and so on. A lot of innovation in law firms over the last few years, for example, has involved interesting and creative ways of applying collaboration and file sharing platforms to clients' issues.

"You know this might not work, right?" – being comfortable with the uncomfortable

The first thing the team, Board, and indeed the firm as a whole has to get their head around is that even if your laterally thinking, curious lawyer who understands their clients and their markets has the best idea in the world, if no one will buy it then, frankly, the idea does not really matter.

We had, we thought, an absolutely brilliant idea in relation to the shortage of lorry drivers in the UK during 2021. The idea came from a conversation with a subject matter expert and a partner who understood their client, and the wider logistics market in particular. The subject matter expert identified an opportunity to help organizations struggling to recruit overseas workers through a novel application of immigration law, which the partner thought clients in the logistics sector could benefit from. We tested the idea with a couple of clients who were keen and mobilized quickly, bringing together a multi-disciplinary team of people – the legal subject matter experts, the innovation team, the people who were going to have to deliver it operationally, and the people that were going to have to sell it. Due to the short window of opportunity, within the space of a fortnight we had a working prototype and two weeks later we had a product ready to sell. We were hugely excited and really proud of what we had achieved and the client was engaged throughout the process. Ultimately, we made two sales, totaling £2,250 – all a bit disheartening. There were a number of reasons why that happened and we learned some lessons as a result, which is the key thing.

Not every bright idea you have is going to work, but it can nevertheless be valuable as long as you take the time to learn the lessons. One of the lessons that we learned was how to mobilize and iterate quickly from idea to prototype to a sellable solution. Even if no one wanted to buy it. Organizationally we learned that there was no problem with experimenting, throwing some time and effort at a project for nothing to come of it – no one was fired or stigmatized as a result. It had all the hallmarks of something that should work and we were excited about its potential, but, ultimately, the market did not want the solution enough. The project also reinforced the need to apply a multi-disciplinary and diverse approach to solving problems. None of us have the monopoly on brilliance, and the killer question that turned something that was going to need an army of paralegals to deliver into a scalable app actually came from the director of the operational function that was going to have to manage the delivery of the solution. Everyone chipped in because this was relevant to their client and not a hypothetical exercise. A colleague who had worked at a well-known cereal company explained that if one in four products that the company tried was successful then, commercially, that was an acceptable rate of return.

There are also ideas that solve a particular client's issue and that, in theory, should be an issue that organizations in the same sector, or even beyond, should also have. This theory can be perfectly sound, but for other organizations the issue simply is not high enough on their agenda of things they need to worry about. You may even have clients who express sufficient interest to sign up for a pilot, with every intention of spending time evaluating the idea (law firms do this to their suppliers and potential suppliers too), but who never quite get around to it. If nothing else, that does tell you something about the urgency of the need (at least for that particular client).

When we started out, having had some demonstrable successes on borrowed time, we wanted to test the Board's appetite to really invest in innovation or whether it was just going to be a bit of lip service. Like all law firms, we have a budgeting process – if we are asking for additional spend, then we are required to make a business case, as you would expect. To test the Board's true interest in innovation, we asked for a six-figure budget for the year. An amount, in the context of our operational spend, that was noticeable but not so noticeable that it amounted to a significant percentage of our overhead. We explained that there was no established business case for it, that we could not explain to the Board what we might spend the money on (albeit we were clearly happy to be held to account for any money we did spend and would at least be able to explain the rationale for the expenditure) and, most importantly, that we might spend the whole budget and have nothing to show for it. This is because that is the reality of establishing an innovation team – or at least it was for us. Over time, we have become more systematic, but we will come to that later.

Forming, storming, norming, and performing – bringing together people with curiosity

So, turning that into some practical steps, where do you start? Firstly, you need to build some capability by putting together a multi-disciplinary team. By this, we do not mean a real estate lawyer, an employment lawyer, a tax lawyer; we mean lawyers, business analysts, project managers, and developers. It may well be, initially, that one person has to perform more than one role (for example, initially our business analyst also performed a project management role). It is not axiomatic that you need lawyers as part of this team; as mentioned in chapter one, there are different views in the market about this. However, to our mind, you should have lawyers as part of your innovation team, at least in the context in which we view innovation – which is fixing both internal problems and those of clients. Not all lawyers are suited to the role, but there are a number of key attributes to look for.

Against a refrain from clients that lawyers (as a wide-sweeping generalization) do not understand their business, there *are* lawyers that excel at that – so have some conversations with those sorts of lawyers. When you have those conversations, use them to gauge how curious the lawyer is. Almost by definition, lawyers who understand their clients' business are inherently curious; they are interested in the client, how their client's business functions, and in providing commercial advice (rather than a treatise on, for example, competition law). Your ideal lawyer in this scenario is one that is able to tell their client things about their business that the client did not already know. Over and above understanding their clients, they also need to understand the wider markets that they are serving so they have an overview of the issues that particular market faces. It is overdone and trite but you are going to need lawyers who are inherently curious – the sort of person who when they get a new smart phone, turn straight to the settings to see what they can change.

They also need to be able to think laterally. If you have a hammer, every solution looks like a nail. If you are a developer, every solution looks like an application. If you are lawyer, every solution looks like legal advice. If you listen to an organization's general counsel who talks about running an in-house team for example, they are usually very clear that, of all the things they have to manage, the requirement for legal advice is just one (often relatively small element) of the overall picture. So, your lawyer needs to be able to think laterally, to think wider than the legal issues facing their clients.

Then you want to get a feel for how comfortable those lawyers are with technology. Not every innovation within a law firm is technology-based, but there is quite often a technology focus. So your curious lawyer who understands their clients (we are taking their legal subject matter expertise as a given) does have to be comfortable with technology. By that, we do not mean they have to be data scientists or software developers, but they do need to understand where technology can help and, as importantly, where it will not provide a solution. Your curious lawyers who have an affinity with technology tend to have a grasp of the capabilities that your firm has, which is where the magic happens and they can join the dots between problems and solutions. We deliberately use the word capability in the context of technology here. For example, the firm may have an NLP, machine-learning tool available – capable of providing a first-pass analysis of large volumes of similar documents, such as leases or derivative contracts. However, understanding the capability is what is important, rather than how to use the product, followed by the ability to think laterally. In a specific example relevant to us, taking the idea of that NLP capability and experimenting with other use cases eventually enabled us to automate file-opening processes on high-volume, low-value work. This conceptual leap might seem obvious, but that is not always the case. We have come across plenty of examples where we show a use case in one particular domain (such as NLP review of large volumes of employment contracts) but, unless the use case is specific to the individual's domain knowledge, they cannot make the conceptual leap that NLP review of employment contracts, *conceptually*, is capable of being applied to leases.

Finally, you need to get a feel for how comfortable they are with uncertainty and failure. Uncertainty and failure are an inherent part of setting up and working in an innovation team and, as a rule, not all lawyers are psychologically equipped to be comfortable with uncertainty and failure (being, as a rule, insecure overachievers[8] with all that that entails). We do not pretend that these people are very common, they may even sound like unicorns – but they do exist, as we can personally attest.

Why are all these attributes important? It comes back to our founding point that we do not innovate in a vacuum. Your curious, technologically adept lawyer, who understands their client and the market they serve, and who can think laterally, can start to identify potential problems that need solving for one or more clients in that market, match their firm's capabilities to those problems and, most importantly, have conversations with clients about whether the ideas they may have about solutions would be ones that the clients would be interested in.

We talked a lot about the qualities of the lawyers specifically in the above paragraphs but curiosity, being technologically adept (if not literate), and comfort with uncertainty and failure are generic qualities that you want from all of your team.

Listen, talk, network, and listen some more – deciding what to do

The successes we have had (and even some of the failures) have all come from subject matter experts who know their clients and know their markets. This comes back to the necessary inherent curiosity, to understand clients' wider challenges, and to see what is happening in the clients' markets; mostly gained from talking to people, networking and most of all listening in order to join the dots – this is where your ideas come from. And you need lots of ideas, because, as we have said, not all of them are going to go anywhere.

So, once you have your ideas, and hopefully you have a surfeit, you need some way of deciding which ones to pursue. Some will be driven by, for example, upcoming tenders and the need to demonstrate internal innovation in your service delivery. Some will come from work that has been done for an existing client to solve issues that other clients are talking about, and will benefit from some time with the innovation team to turn it in to something more consistent and more like a product (with a pricing mechanism and similar). Other ideas may be more speculative, and these can be more problematic – particularly for your sales team, where your sales team are, *de facto*, the partners in your firm.

Our experience is that a lot of lawyers are uncomfortable going to clients with an idea short of a beautifully formed and finished article, or indeed an idea in which their client might not be interested. As a rule, they want to be able to be right, and to provide the client with the answer. However, there is an arrogance in that approach when it comes to innovation as it assumes that the lawyer is capable of completely defining the problem and presenting the fully formed solution to the client. There is a whole chicken-and-egg thing that needs resolving. The lawyers will not talk to the clients until they have something to show them, and the innovation team who have any number of competing priorities do not want to invest time and effort (and a proportion of the unallocated budget) on something that the clients may not want. But this is essential, you have to do some market testing (keeping in mind that people will not always say what they are thinking and, indeed, do not always do what they say they will) and for law firms that market testing is largely about talking to clients. It is outside of the comfort zone for many lawyers to do this, which is fine and to be expected, in which case the key becomes persuading the partners to bring along to meetings with clients one of your innovation team who can then have those conversations. We have had situations where we have been asked to speak to a client as they stated a particular need, but upon discussion and some probing, it transpired that was not their biggest issue, which is the one we instead helped them to solve (*"the unspoken known"*).

Once you have had some conversations with clients who seem to think that the idea is worthwhile then, assuming they are not simply being polite, you need to be able to find some clients who will engage with you to develop the idea. You may have to start with a minimal viable product (ideally a client will have helped develop this with you) to help with the next stage of the conversation. Once again, part of the reason for doing this is calling the clients' bluff, to an extent. If this is a real issue for them that they want solving, then they should be willing to invest some time on the solution. If you cannot find any clients who have the time to engage at this stage, then we would argue that it probably is not enough of a problem for clients to want to spend money on the solution. All organizations have all sorts of things going on at any given time and only a finite amount of resource to apply – if your idea is not one of the things they see value in applying time to, then you have to at least question whether it is a solution that is commercially viable.

It's not just about the technology – starting the hearts and minds journey

You now have a bunch of curious, (largely) resilient, technologically adept lawyers on your team. You are going to have to invest in that team, develop them, and allow them the time and space to practice the skills needed to bring ideas, innovations, and products to market. They are the ones that are going to have to help the partners who are less comfortable talking to clients outside of their subject matter expertise.

In terms of hearts and minds, it helps those partners who sit outside of the innovation team if they can deal with the lawyers from the innovation team. It is one less barrier to overcome, talking lawyer to lawyer as it were. They speak the language and have had the same experiences (broadly – though the number of lawyers in one domain who say of a lawyer in another domain, "I have no idea what you do" is somewhat baffling to our mind, but there you go).

The evolution of our innovation team came as a result of some of our successes. We suddenly found ourselves with innovations or products that were being used, without really any way of managing the product lifecycle (amongst other things). In many instances we were, to be frank, successful in spite of ourselves rather than because of, but, during that journey, we learned a number of lessons around what worked and what did not (for us). We started to systematize the product lifecycle from idea to execution, and we started to build methodologies – a standard operating procedure for identifying the ideas we wanted to pursue; and one around our go-to-market approach, for how we tracked and understood the sales effort involved in each of the products that we developed.

Ultimately, that evolution spawned our product and innovation department. The department was made up of six product and innovation partners, aligned to six (of the seven) segments that we present to the market, namely insurance, public sector, health, built environment, corporates, and owner-managed businesses. Each of those partners fulfilled the criteria we talked about above, with the role to help their segments develop and take ideas and products to market, becoming product managers for their particular segments. Product lifecycles and selling products is quite different to selling services so we hired a product manager from outside of the industry (albeit with a law degree) to help us build our methodology, as well as to coach and mentor the product and innovation partners so they could fulfil their role as product managers in their segments.

Case study – bAIley

Challenge/opportunity

The innovation team included lawyers, developers, business analysts, and legal engineers. It was formed of a group of people who had never worked together before and, as the team was newly formed, it was important to work on a project to which everyone could contribute. Whilst the team were responsible for conceiving, championing, and carefully developing approaches that had not been tried in the firm before, colleagues were key to the program of growth and evolution. We knew that in order to be a successful team and help our clients, the innovation team needed to ensure colleagues were brought on this "journey".

The first step in encouraging a culture of innovation was to show it in action, and the team came up with the idea of a chatbot to help bring this brave new world to life. AI and innovation can often appear quite detached from the day-to-day work of a legal professional, so our innovation team was keen to provide a practical example of how we could use AI that was of real value to people, and to personalize how we delivered our messages and received ideas. We also wanted to use this as an internal proof of concept for chatbots, a pilot project with the ultimate view to finding use cases for our clients. Finally, we were looking for something that would not cost much and could be up and running quickly, which was possible as it was built on Microsoft's QnA Maker.

Strategy

There is a constant demand on our business service teams to deal with a high proportion of what are, in essence, routine or generic queries from colleagues, usually along the lines of "*How do I do X, Y, or Z?*". Ideally, we wanted to provide people with their own personal instant assistant that they could call upon when they had a question. That way they get an answer at the point of need, enabling them to fulfil a task quickly and easily, rather than having to research who or what can help, contact another department and, inevitably, wait for a response – slowing them down and inconveniencing both them and the recipient, ultimately, interrupting everybody's workflow.

To solve the instant assistant problem, we created bAIley – a gender-neutral chatbot charged with answering generic questions and guiding people to the help they need. bAIley launched in May 2018 – it was initially loaded with HR queries, but has since expanded into marketing, facilities, expert signposting ("who knows what"), and finance. Not satisfied with just that, bAIley encourages others to be enterprising, acting as the receptacle for innovation ideas.

bAIley soon became the internal "spokesperson" for innovation – a messenger for all things innovative (including AI) at Weightmans. bAIley provided updates on our activities, conducted surveys, and had an electronic bookshelf to store the updates. The innovation team conducted a national roadshow, taking with them a life-size cutout of bAIley to tour the offices and to share technology news. We even added bAIley to our HR system so bAIley was available as a contact on our internal directory.

People

In and of itself, the exercise was great for generating team spirit in the newly formed innovation team and with colleagues in other departments (marketing, HR, and IT in particular), not least because the night before launch there were several members still logged on at 1am to deal with some technical issues in relation to sizing when we moved it from the test servers into production.

Getting endorsement and support from the relevant teams was vital to the success of the project, and we made sure they were involved throughout the project. We had to design the character who would be the face of our chatbot and then work out how best to deploy the technology within our infrastructure in a manner that was user friendly. Design for a chatbot is very important to ensure a positive user experience, and our team had to consider everything, from how much of the screen it takes up, to where it is launched from.

Execution

bAIley was planned by members of the innovation team over a six-week period, with the design, information collection, and technical aspects all worked on simultaneously. We worked in tandem with a local design agency to create the gender-neutral character and subsequently trademarked bAIley.

On 31 May 2018, the bAIley chatbot was launched across the firm by way of a (rare) desktop wallpaper takeover and an all-user email introducing bAIley (by bAIley). The first release of bAIley focused on HR functionality as this leant itself to a high volume of routine queries. We also had some team call guides, generic internal information (such as reception phone numbers), generic chatbot questions, and some "just for fun" responses such as a favorite color and the occasional joke to encourage people to engage with it.

The firm holds a monthly welcome day for new recruits and, as part of the innovation session, the legal engineers introduce bAIley, as a lot of the functionality assists new starters to settle in and find the information they need. The typical HR questions asked by new recruits had been collated as they were indicative of the questions that were routinely asked of the HR inbox. bAIley's knowledge base is regularly updated to be reflective of the range of queries asked and to ensure the answers are correct. In terms of HR queries, we are delighted that it can correctly answer 84 percent of the questions.

We also reviewed the questions that bAIley cannot currently answer to identify future information we can add, and this has influenced the order in which we have added knowledge to bAIley. One of the legal engineers has taken charge of updating the knowledge bases for bAIley, regularly interacting with other teams to improve bAIley's knowledge. Engagement with bAIley has been high, thousands of questions have been asked (5,136 in the first 12 months) and successfully answered. Some of the more amusing questions that bAIley has been asked include, "What do you think of the likelihood of a robot take over?" and "How do you measure your self-worth?". We have also shown bAIley to clients, as a way of them alleviating some of the same internal business problems that we had, or as a way of us sharing information about each other, so that clients could ask who the contact would be for a particular area of work or the chatbot could assist with some specific knowledge queries, for example around General Data Protection Regulation (GDPR).

Outcome

In the first 12 months, bAIley was asked 5,136 queries. If each query just saved one unit of time (a conservative estimate), this is a time saving of 513 hours – meaning people get the information they want much faster and freeing up other staff from dealing with routine queries for more complex ones. bAIley has been well received by people across different teams and levels of experience, including our managing partner, who asked bAIley a question and could not hide his surprise that he got the correct answer in response! We were keen to ensure the design for bAIley was friendly to allay any misplaced fears of a robot take over, and bAIley became a recognized internal brand as the face of our innovation and on our laptop skins.

The expertise signposting functionality was added as a direct request by a Board member. When an individual within Weightmans is working on a file, if they need assistance with an area of law, up until bAIley we did not have a straightforward way of seeing which specialisms other members of staff have. At best, finding this information required asking colleagues, or cold-calling internal departments.

In November 2018, the bAIley release focused on an improved layout of the information that bAIley can display, including contact cards for people, enabling a dynamic response to queries relating to staff and their skills. bAIley has also been key to growing the firm-wide presence of the innovation team as the icon is on everyone's desktop and bAIley has an email address too. This approach has led to far more people than we anticipated suggesting ideas and innovative solutions, enabling us to increase the size of the innovation team and create new roles, such as legal engineer. This, in turn, resulted in more projects and ideas to explore and less time to focus on bAIley, despite ambitious plans. However, recent advances in generative AI means this is something we are hoping to resurrect.

What did we learn?

- *Do not overlook the aesthetic.* Design, even for a chatbot, is very important – especially in terms of how much of a screen it takes up and where it is launched from.
- *Be careful how you say no.* The "no answer" messaging is also very important – and this needs to be updated along with topics added.
- *Spare resources for the launch.* Keeping the responses up to date around launch is time intensive. When launching a chatbot, you need to have people logged on for the first couple of days, regularly updating the knowledge base in order to be able to answer the questions asked, and also providing some amusing answers to some of the more unusual questions asked.
- *Knowledge is power.* Keeping the knowledge base up to date is key. Make sure that the initial information collection also looks forward to any key issues or seasonal variations so that the initial accuracy is even higher.

Chapter checklist

- ☐ What is your reason for innovating? Is this a universally held view in your organization? What are the nuances?
- ☐ Are you starting from scratch or picking up a half-started innovation process?
- ☐ What is your approach to innovation – do you want to be at the forefront of innovation, a fast follower, or a late adopter? Does your approach vary depending on the area of work, type of technology, or level of risk?
- ☐ What is (are) the problem(s) you are trying to solve? Are they sufficiently understood? How do you decide what to do first?
- ☐ Who can help you internally and externally – do you need to expand your innovation network? Who might want to work on this with you? Can you borrow people to get started?
- ☐ What level of senior buy-in for innovation do you have?
- ☐ What will success look like?
- ☐ What are your support systems and who are your cheerleaders? This work is hard and a lot of things will fail – how comfortable is your organization with failure?
- ☐ How can you engage the hearts and minds in your organization?

References

1 Redaction tools based on natural language processing (NLP) and predictive reserving – a solution that we continued to invest in once the funding ran out, and indeed continue to develop to this day.

2 Al-Abdulkarim, L., Atkinson, K., Bench-Capon, T., Whittle, S., Williams, R., and Wolfenden, C., "Noise Induced Hearing Loss: An Application of the Angelic Methodology", *Legal Knowledge and Information Systems*, Volume 302, 2017. Al-Abdulkarim, L., Atkinson, K., Bench-Capon, T., Whittle, S., Williams, R., and Wolfenden, C., "Noise induced hearing loss: Building an application using the ANGELIC methodology", *Argument & Computation*, Volume 10 (1), 2019. See: https://content.iospress.com/articles/argument-and-computation/aac181005. Atkinson, K., Bench-Capon, T., Routen, T., Sanchez, A., Whittle, S., Williams, R., and Wolfenden, C., "Realising ANGELIC designs using logiak", *Legal Knowledge and Information Systems: JURIX 2019: The Thirty-second Annual Conference*, Volume 322, 2019. See https://livrepository.liverpool.ac.uk/id/eprint/3081251.

3 Although do not underestimate the amount of time spent unpicking the rough and ready processes, especially if you then try and tie it in with product – see chapter 12.

4 It is our firm view that the successful law firms of the future will be those that are

able to put together multi-disciplinary teams of people who can help design solutions for clients, only part of which may need formal, traditional, legal input.

5 An unsustainable number, in our opinion.

6 Flood, H., "Getting more from George R. R. Martin", 14 April 2011. See: www.theguardian.com/books/booksblog/2011/apr/14/more-george-r-r-martin.

7 Accepting that the Henry Ford quote is probably apocryphal.

8 "Insecure Overachievers", BBC Radio 4, 26 September 2018. See: www.bbc.co.uk/programmes/b0bkqy1l.

Chapter 3: Getting started – proofs of concepts and methodologies

As with most things in life, getting started is hard, especially if you are essentially staring at a blank piece of paper. Our early days working on innovation were really hard. Everyone was looking at us to come up with a plan, but we did not know how best to do it and certainly had no formal training – which comes as quite a shock when you are used to the innate rhythm of being a lawyer where your time is structured by the safety of six-minute units. Whilst lawyers will typically bemoan the tyranny of hitting hours and revenue targets, those targets do become a scaffold for your working life and their absence can leave you feeling entirely rudderless. At the beginning, it all felt quite piecemeal and reactive – with some reflection and experience you realize that few of the processes you implement at the beginning will survive or scale and, much as you will innovate on projects, you will innovate fairly constantly on your own governance and processes around innovation.

The ideation process – creating a hopper of ideas

Once you have decided to get going and have a bit of time, you obviously need some ideas to work on. When we were doing this as part-time endeavors around existing roles, if we are entirely honest, we started on something that we both wanted to do. In a moment of serendipity in 2016, we had both independently come across Professor Katie Atkinson – Stuart at a conference and then on a train journey back North, and Catriona via an article in *The Law Society Gazette*[1] – and thought that we must be able to apply Professor Atkinson's work on modelling legal reasoning from academic papers onto actual cases, so we set off to boil that ocean.[2] This idea was all about using computer systems to support legal reasoning (as after all, law can often be boiled down to "if this, then that", which is what you need for a computer system). Luckily for us, as we were based in Liverpool it was a pleasant stroll up Brownlow Hill to the leafy quadrangle where the University of Liverpool's Computer Science Department was based. Even luckier, Professor Atkinson was very generous with her time and was able to explain her complex work in such a way that we understood the gist and could then think about practical use cases, on which we then all collaborated.

You will often hear talk of working on quick wins and getting the "low hanging fruit" – suggestions aimed at gaining some momentum and being able to quickly show some value or outcomes to your organization, with the hope that this will then result in more people, budget, or time. This is often a sensible approach but one we, in our infinite wisdom, ignored, wanting more of a big bang to start us off. Our success was two hard years in the making where we learned a lot, including how best to collaborate with academia.[3] With hindsight, and being entirely candid, we started out far too big but as we did have some success,[4] we gained interest within our organization. Importantly, it provided the opportunity to present a business case to the Board, saying that in order to do this project properly, the firm needed to invest in it and, in particular, it needed people and resources to continue. This was when the role of innovation manager was created and we recruited two internal legal engineers and seconded a business analyst – we had started to form our own pirates in the navy.[5] As mentioned in chapter two, the key test for us as to how serious the Board were in terms of investing in innovation, beyond the creation of a team, was the allocation of a budget where, in contrast to pretty much every other line in our annual financial budget, we were saying to the Board that:

- We would like a reasonable pot of money to enable us to experiment;
- We cannot tell you, at the time of budgeting, what we might be spending it on;
- We cannot tell you what return you will get from any spend; and
- Indeed, we cannot guarantee that you will get any return at all, as that is the nature of innovation.

Our firm has a strong history in insurance work, which has meant that over many years our clients requested that we capture a lot of discrete data points on a matter-by-matter basis that we could roll up to portfolio level,[6] so they can look at lifecycle, indemnity spend, and reserving. This often involved turning unstructured data into structured data, which was then inputted into our case management system (CMS). In turn, the CMS fed our data warehouse, which brought together multiple data sources (our financial system, HR system, and CRM system in particular) to enable us to combine those data sources in a holistic view. Turning unstructured data into structured data was essentially a manual task that our case handlers would have to do by, for example, reading a medical report, extracting the likely prognosis, and then typing that prognosis into a data field in the CMS.

Depending on the type of work and a client's particular requirements, there could be anything up to 250 data fields that our case handlers were required to complete for each individual matter. As a manual task it suffered a couple of issues – our case handlers seemed not to be particularly enamored with the idea of being data-entry clerks (that was not what they thought being a lawyer was going to be about),[7] and we also had data quality issues (inevitable human error). So, in our heads, a logical step was to ask whether we could use technology to extract those structured data fields from unstructured documents. Could we a) remove the burden from case handlers, b) improve the data quality in the process, and c) could we capture even more data than we already did (as an added bonus). Then, could we build a decision-support tool that mapped out all of the possible permeations in a legal domain? Several peer-reviewed academic papers later, and we have shown that we can.[8]

We commenced the project with The University of Liverpool on a shoestring budget, but great support in terms of buy in, which started to create interest within the firm in what we might do next. We did what, with hindsight, was not the most effective method of generating ideas – we asked people to put innovation suggestions into our online recognition platform, but did not set any parameters around the types of ideas we wanted. We also toured the offices with a seven-foot cardboard cut-out (fun to carry on a train!) of our chatbot mascot, bAIley,[9] with a suggestion box (both virtual and physical) for people to share ideas. What quickly became apparent was what we thought of as innovation was not what the rest of the firm thought of as innovation: we got a lot of ideas around (waste) bins and core IT systems, which we redirected to the relevant business services team. In future idea-collection events, we changed our approach, instead suggesting buckets of innovation themes that people might like to think of use cases for. We talked around our capabilities, such as automation or decision support, and gave an example to help inspire people – preferably something we had done with a client to show the benefits of getting involved. This became a much more useful way of sourcing ideas.

We have also got better at bouncing around our organization (virtually or in person), showing and telling people what we are doing and essentially being our own PR. In the early days, when the team was very small, this was a difficult balance between the actual "doing of innovation" and talking to the firm about what we were doing – the act of talking, by necessity, stopping the actual work. You will also probably find that the people who are interested in the activity of innovation are less keen on talking (and so that became a role we carried out). This, in part, informed our thinking when we were creating the role of product and innovation partner, and the types of things we wanted them to do. We continually evolve how we communicate activities, currently using intranet pages, the internal weekly newsletter, show and tell sessions, workshops and team/department meetings as a way to share our work and approach and source ideas. We tie our discussions into our firm's vision and values which, usefully for us, can be encapsulated as "See The Possibility".[10] We have found, as a rule, that you cannot communicate too much in this regard. Importantly, we share the same message to the entire firm, so our new apprentices get the same set of slides on what we are working on as our Board. Although both groups ask very different questions, they both receive the same core message – nothing dilutes innovation messages quicker than people only hearing half of something and taking it as complete. An observation that is universally true and not just limited to innovation.

Does it solve a problem and is it doable? Prioritizing ideas

At some stage, and usually much sooner that you expect, you will have more ideas than you have available time, budget, or people, not least because innovation teams are always keen to hear new ideas and encourage people to speak with them. You then need to be able to prioritize those ideas so that you can focus efforts on what is important to your organization. This is not as simple as it sounds, particularly in a law firm where there can be many political undercurrents to maneuver.

Before you leap into the prioritization process though, you need to ensure that you are clear enough on what the ideas actually are so that you have an idea of impact, timescale, and resource. Stuart is a particular champion of the phrase, "What is the problem you are trying to solve?" and one of these days, we will buy him a t-shirt with it on. It is, however, a very good question to ask as it makes people think about what their idea is trying to help with and, crucially, how they can articulate this to others (similar to an elevator pitch). What might be clear in someone's head who has literally been living and breathing the concept can get lost in translation when they try to explain it to someone else. In addition, our experience is that people have a tendency to demand a specific solution based largely on their own knowledge and experience which, typically for a lawyer, can be limited in domains other than the law (in which their experience and knowledge runs deep). So rather than starting with the solution, we want the actual problem.

To mitigate this risk, we implemented formal 15-minute discovery sessions between the person who had the idea and members of the product and innovation department to do an initial stress test of the idea – this usually results in some homework for the person with the idea, which also helps to sift out those who, for whatever reason, are unlikely to have the time to commit to the project. If they cannot invest the time at this stage, they are unlikely to be able to invest the time when the project becomes more involved. We also use it to dismiss the notion that simply throwing your idea to the innovation team is all that is needed for it to magically happen. After this, a longer vision session is held if the idea has merit and meets other criteria (which would be specific to the organization).

How you choose to "score" ideas for deciding priority will differ from firm to firm and is likely to be based on other methods that may already exist within your organization – perhaps in IT, marketing, or projects teams. It is important to remember when implementing a scoring system that you've also got to bring your organization on the innovation process "journey" with you. Not only are you asking them to do what they perceive as unfamiliar things in running innovation projects, you are potentially wanting to implement a whole new way of doing them and the potential for change overload exists. As we started, we inherited a business change project request form. As you might expect, this was not wholly fit for our purpose, but having been told to use it, we did (for a short while at least, before we modified it).

The problem with the form was that you scored highly (to the extent that the weighting was affected for pretty much every other question) for saying the project would win new work or prevent it from being lost. Lawyers, not ones to miss a loophole, had spotted this – meaning this became the default answer and all the ideas scored the same, thereby defeating the object of scoring to prioritize. Keen to retain the familiarity of the project request form, we amended the scoring in the background (and hid the scoring). We made the scoring more nuanced – looking at the scale of the project, cost, people, and availability – all with subcategories that were scored differently. A maximum of two ideas at any one time could have additional points awarded because the idea was deemed especially important to pursue. We therefore were able to separate out ideas in terms of scores and report back on why one idea was ahead of another to partners who had been more used to asking for something and getting it, rather than having the request prioritized at a firm-wide level.

When we combined product and innovation into one department in May

2022, we took the opportunity to align the way ideas and products were prioritized and the scoring matrix has become more nuanced, including alignment with ESG values, for example. However you choose to prioritize ideas, it will never be perfect and will evolve, but at least you will have some mechanism and rationalization that shows how you came up with the order of priority and proves it was not done on a whim.

In the product world, we ask our segment heads[11] to suggest a prioritization list for their area, which we then compare with our scoring. Any discrepancies are discussed until an agreement is reached at segment level. We then review all the segment priorities, available resources (time, budget, people) and come up with a list across the firm where the ideas are placed in tranches (rather than in competition with each other, which helps how this is received internally). Ideas in tranche one are the highest priority and are worked on in preference to the other tranches; if there are no outstanding actions on a tranche one project then the team would start to pick up tasks from projects in tranche two, and so on. Of course, innovation is, by its very nature, dynamic, so some reprioritization is needed throughout the year, which in turn necessitates moving projects up and down the tranches or putting them on hold, all of which needs communicating back to the organization. In terms of managing your stakeholders, communication is the key and, to repeat, our general experience is you cannot communicate too much.

The execution of ideas is always a concern for those tasked with implementing and managing innovation. Balancing an innovation portfolio of quick wins, longer term strategic/blue sky projects and a spread of projects between departments or segments is a persistent challenge, and one where you have to accept that you are never going to please everyone. The balancing act is very similar to how you have to work as a lawyer, where you are working on multiple matters for multiple clients at the same time (and making each client feel as if they are your only client). When you start out, it is hard to know how many projects can be live at any one time but, by a process of trial and error, this improves over the years as you get better at:

- Understanding new technologies, with members of a team developing real expertise in them so that the actual execution speeds up.
- Estimating how much input you need (and when) from a subject matter expert so you can factor in an average amount of delay when these experts, who are invariably lawyers, have to concentrate on the day job.
- Working out which other departments you need to collaborate with –

the more departments involved, the more the lifecycle seems to increase exponentially unless you have very strict project management around it.

- Allowing the innovation team some time to experiment and learn – for example, Google famously used the "80/20 rule" where 20 percent of time was allowed for side projects. We are not sure that it needs to be that formal, but it is important to have some time just to experiment and have some skunkworks projects – this may be doing new things on existing technology or trying out new ideas where it is accepted that it is ok to fail.

Running a pilot – from timing and success criteria to risk approval and everything in between

Although innovation is not always about technology, it often plays a role. In our example (discussed above) with the University of Liverpool, we knew that once we had been able to map out an area of law in such a way that a computer system could be used to support the legal reasoning then we would need technology that gave us the capability to:

- Review unstructured documents and extract structured data.
- Build the legal reasoning into a system that was easy for lawyers to interact with and did not require a lot of IT team resource.

We watched a number of demos and narrowed the options down to a handful of pilots for the University of Liverpool project. We learned the hard way that there are many factors that affect the success of pilots and summarize them for you in this section.

Make my problem go away

As an innovation team and as a group of end users who are usually lawyers, you all have the same end goal in mind – to make the problem go away. Realistically, there is unlikely to be one solution that works for everyone all of the time, and getting half of the way to solving the problem should be considered as a win. It is always worth taking the time to explore and document the problem so that everyone is on the same page (documentation is especially key for later reference) and checking as the project progresses that the problem, and everyone's understanding of it, has not changed as people's thought processes evolve over time.

A common challenge is delivering solutions that fall short of perfect. The point we try and emphasize is that there is no such thing as completely perfect, so the question should be, "Have we made things better or worse?". If the former (i.e. we have made something better), then that is something we can build on.

Timing

The timing of a pilot can make or break its success. As a general rule, there is no good time for a pilot, but there are times that are worse than others. The times that are best avoided include:

- Ends of months, quarters, years, or any other period that relates to billing in your organization as the focus is, rightly, on other things.
- Close to other roll-outs, which could be related to technology, marketing, process, or finance changes – you do not want to contribute to roll-out fatigue.
- Periods of instability in the relevant team – this could be in terms of starters and leavers, a change in the law, or onboarding a new client.
- Times when the other teams (often business services, such as IT) that you need to be involved in your pilot are thin on the ground or dealing with other time-critical projects.

Scope

In addition to setting out the problem you are trying to solve with the pilot, it is important to set out the scope, which sets out the boundaries for it (in particular, the things you aren't going to do as part of the pilot), the outcome sought, and how this will be measured. This can be done in multiple ways, but a straightforward one can involve covering:

- Questions the pilot can answer;
- Questions the pilot cannot answer; and
- Questions we are not looking for the pilot to answer.

This can also be referred to as the pilot progresses to ensure there is no scope creep, which may affect the problem you are trying to solve.

Demos

You quickly realize after seeing a handful of demos that not all are equal. The best offerings tend to:

- Involve a pre-demo call to tailor the demo to your use cases and problems;

- Make it easy for you to run a pilot with them;
- Handle an invitation to tender or pre-qualification questionnaire and have information readily available;
- Have done their research on your organization and the sector and come equipped with ideas;
- Demonstrate that they are in it for the long haul and can point to customers with whom they actively collaborate;
- Not be delivered as if it is a training session;
- Not tell you the whole history of the company for the last goodness knows how many years,
- Invite all participants to ask questions and be involved in the discussion, not just the most senior;
- Not feature damaging personal bias (such as assuming the man in the room is the decision maker);
- Ask about your timescales and do not chase everyone on the call (or indeed your boss or another partner who was not); and
- Not go directly to the lawyers as this just irritates and hampers the IT and innovation teams, who then have to spend time backtracking.

It will not come as a surprise that poorer demos are usually the exact opposite. We usually use the innovation team as the first round filter for demos and if one looks promising, we then ask a couple of lawyers who would be ultimate users to attend another shorter demo session. If there are a couple of potential solutions that look viable, we aim to line them up close to each other so it is easier to compare them.

Budget

Innovation teams, especially in the early days, often work on a limited budget. Paying for a pilot can eat into that, which means that fewer pilots can proceed. However, there are some advantages to a paid pilot – it can help make lawyer resource available to ensure the pilot can go ahead (sometimes a free pilot is never deemed a high enough priority), and indeed can assist with freeing up the time of other internal teams needed to support the pilot, such as IT or risk and compliance. It can also ensure that you receive more assistance from the supplier and it is often offset against the purchase price if you proceed.

Risk and compliance

Once you have completed several pilots, you are likely to know the right time to involve your risk and compliance team, but when you are a new team then involving them as early as possible is best, in our experience. There is nothing worse than thinking you have everything ready for a pilot and then realizing there is a piece of information required by your risk and compliance team missing. We developed a pilot planning checklist (which is included at the end of this chapter), which means that the whole innovation team can be involved and see what is left to complete. We complete, and then keep under review, the information security and Data Privacy Impact Assessment documents at the earliest opportunity and ask our risk team to review the final terms should we proceed. This is because your risk team are likely to have some requirements (for example around data locations or a specific contractual term) and it is best to know these in advance or in the pilot preparation stage as there is no point in running a pilot for something you cannot proceed with. Do not underestimate how long it can take to perform the necessary governance steps (often multiple times the length of the actual pilot). Again, this plays into the timing point – if it takes eight weeks to agree the governance documents, this needs to be included in working out when the pilot begins to avoid it overlapping with one of the times we mentioned.

What are you using as the test case?

Depending on the attitude of your risk and compliance team, the type of materials you can use in a pilot typically need to be ascertained early on so that, if necessary, they can be obtained or created. We made sets of example documents for the purposes of some pilots, in part so we could see how different systems worked with the same set of information, and in part to satisfy our risk and compliance team. However, it is a slow process making realistic example documents. If you are using real documents or materials, then you need to be clear on the type of information you need, for example on a particular point of law, in a certain jurisdiction, or up to a set value. You then need to work with the lawyers to see how much of the right kind of information is available, or how frequently it arises, so you can factor that in to how long the pilot should take and who needs to be involved.

People

You clearly need to choose your pilot group carefully. You need:

- People who are willing to test something;
- People who accept that it is a pilot and might not be perfect;
- People who can see that the solution at least has the potential of solving a problem for them or their clients;
- Diversity, with a full range of experiences from beginners to experts as they will all spot different things with the technology;
- People who are prepared to sacrifice their time to help with the pilot and evaluate it; and
- People who work in a reasonably consistent manner, or at least in a reasonably consistent way for the part of the work that the innovation is a proposed solution for.

In an organization obsessed by time and by measuring its expenditure, these people can be hard to come by. You will need to get your senior stakeholders on board first as they are responsible for the people who you are asking to be involved. If your senior stakeholders aren't on board then you need to find a different pilot group with a senior stakeholder who is.

There is some merit in involving skeptics in a pilot as it does help you plan for any barriers you may face with the eventual adoption, but you need to know who the skeptics are before the pilot starts and not have too many in the group. There is no perfect solution, even if everyone could agree on the definition of perfect; further to this lawyers are, by training and nature, predisposed to (and take great delight in) pointing out all of the ways that something is not perfect. The first couple of times you run a pilot you may wish to avoid including skeptics while you are gaining experience on running and managing the pilot process. You will not want their skepticism to detract from the hard work your innovation team has done in getting to the pilot stage, much of which is behind the scenes and unnoticed. It can be pretty demotivating for the innovation team if their first contact with a pilot group results in their work being torn to shreds.

As with all change, it is important to make sure your messaging is clear, especially in relation to the benefits it brings to the end user and the problem it solves for them. No one wants a pile of technical jargon to wade through to work out why they should adopt the solution.

Success criteria

Success criteria help you work out if the technology solves the problem you have set out to address and should be agreed upfront – we tend to limit the number to three or four as any more than that and you are left trying to work out where the line is drawn to count something as a success. The suppliers are often very keen to help draft these with you, which you should embrace as their experience will be helpful. We encourage at least one or two quantitative, more objective, measures such as around time, cost, enhanced accuracy, or consistency (and do not be afraid to ask the supplier what figures similar organizations have obtained) and then some around ease of use, trust, or confidence in using the system or the outcome.

Trying multiple use cases

Ideally, solutions that will work for as much of the organization as possible to gain efficiencies in terms of cost, training, developing systems, and dealing with queries are good ones to start with. This does mean that sometimes you need multiple pilot groups all trying different use cases, which in an ideal world you would look to run at the same time. For best results, you want the use cases to be as different and as extreme as possible on the basis that if it works for those groups, it should work for use cases in the middle. This means a lot of work for the innovation team and there may be times where it makes more sense to run the use cases sequentially, so that feedback from the first users can be incorporated into the training for the next group. In that scenario, it usually makes sense to start with the more straightforward use case first.

Training

There is likely to be training required before the pilot users are let loose on the technology in question. Whether the training is done by the supplier or by the innovation team, you want to make sure it is as relevant to the end users as possible, takes as little time as possible, and is as close to the user's actual use of the technology as possible. i.e. make the training contextually relevant rather than a trawl through all the available features. If, for example, there are functions that most users are never going to use, training them on this just detracts from the areas they will use and makes the solution appear more complicated and less user friendly. We are often admonished, "Just tell me what I need to know". In this scenario, consider separating the training according to functionality required and run additional sessions for the few that will need the edge features and functionality. It can sometimes be useful to run training just with more junior colleagues so they are happy asking questions without partners present, and separate training for partners who may not want to ask questions they are concerned are low-level in front of more junior colleagues (or indeed in front of other partners – it can be a good investment of time to train partners individually). Regardless of who is delivering the training, you want to make sure that the innovation team understands the system well so they can be the first port of call for any queries. Refresher training can be useful as not everyone will use the system immediately and when they eventually do come to use it they will likely need a bit of help. Where we can, we provide example documents or scenarios as part of the training so they get to interact with the system rather than just passively watch training.

Feedback

Before the pilot commences, you need to plan how you will collect feedback from the users. This could be:

- Surveys sent out at various stages of the pilot;
- One on one interviews; and/or
- A group feedback session.

Feedback clearly needs to cover questions that ascertain the extent to which the target problem has been solved. It is also useful to capture feedback on the level of experience of the user (for example, are they a newly qualified solicitor or a partner) as this can affect their views of the solution's success. It is useful to have a mix of qualitative and quantitative feedback so that you can compare pilots and products against each other. Questions around the perception of trust in any system or outcome should be captured so that they can be tracked over time to see if the culture is changing. Sometimes, pilots can have unintended consequences that can be positive or negative so some free text questions that look to capture this are also useful. Once the pilot has concluded, it often helps with the hearts and minds struggle to share a summary of the outcome of the pilot and the next steps.

How long should a pilot last?

Pilot lengths depend on the type of technology involved, alongside a combination of other factors including;

- The time of year – we mentioned timing above in terms of avoiding key business dates like the end of the financial year, but you also need to factor in any holiday periods. You do not want to train people who might end up needing retraining after their holiday, or who are busy finishing things the week before, or catching up afterwards – all of which means that they can be out of action for four weeks of any pilot period. You also do not want your key contact at the supplier company to be away for the pilot as this makes dealing with any problems that much harder.

- If you are training on example data or materials, then a shorter pilot period often works best as otherwise people will just put off trying the system right until the end of the time period, where they often run out of time or materials to review.
- If you are using live data or materials, then the pilot needs to be long enough for the type of use case you need to arise, ideally multiple times and for all of the people in the pilot group.
- Ensure the pilot is short enough to instill some sense of urgency around trying the systems over the course of the pilot, rather than a lot of use in the final week.
- Ensure the pilot is long enough for the time spent by the lawyers on training and any other pre-pilot preparation to feel worth it.
- Ensure the period is long enough for the lawyers to use the system on multiple occasions so if, for example, you are looking at potential time savings, then you are getting representative data of someone familiar with the system rather than just someone's first, often slower, attempt.

All of these factors usually mean that a pilot lasts between four and eight weeks.

How many pilots?

Depending on the problem to be solved, you may want to run multiple pilots of similar products in order to pick one. There are several factors to consider when exploring this approach:

- Can the pilots run at the same time, or do they need to be sequential? This is usually determined by whether you need to use the same group of lawyers. If you do, how do you ensure the material used in the pilots is the same or similar if you are not using example data?
- If sequential, and the same group of people are needed, consider if the data collected, for example on time savings, is a result of the product itself or a result of the lawyer being more familiar with the type of product (or a combination of both).
- How are you going to decide which product to proceed with? How

much weight are you giving to user feedback compared to cost, for example?

- If you pilot multiple products using the same group of people, the product they usually want is the mythical unicorn that doesn't exist and combines the best features of the different products – that can mean a conversation with the supplier to see how receptive they are to user-generated enhancements to their products.

Dealing with the inevitable hiccups

There are inevitably hiccups when running pilots. This is to be expected and does not usually affect the overall outcome if they are dealt with well. For this, a system is needed for users to request help with queries or get refresher training. In our early days, this was just asking the pilot group to phone us, but, with more projects and pilots all running at the same time, this needs to become a bit more systemized. We have found that a shared team email address, with emails categorized by a color for each member of the team to avoid duplicating efforts, works well and has the added advantage of being simple to set up. With most pilots, anyone in the innovation team should have enough knowledge of the technology to act as a first line of response and you can often share template responses around any common issues. If there are more nuanced queries, then you may escalate this within the team before liaising with the external provider. It often helps for the innovation team to have pre-established check-in calls with the external provider to feed back any issues and to get any tips that can help with the rest of the pilot. You may also be able to use a separate instance of your IT team's help desk software to manage incoming requests for assistance.

Adoption and roll-out

We discuss this in chapter nine – suffice it to say for now that a successful pilot is just the start!

Delivering a pilot to a client

The first time you deliver a pilot where you are the supplier and a client is the user is a bit of a heart-stopping moment, although usually by that stage you have been on the receiving end of multiple pilots and demos and have made your mental list of what works and what does not. You need to put that list into practice and help the client to plan the pilot, being sensitive to how experienced, or not, they may be at running pilots themselves. Liaising with the client's change team is important as you can often help them with the messaging, especially if it is a tool you have tried and tested internally. When acting as the supplier, you need to make sure you have your governance in good order so that you can answer any data or information security questions that come your way, and have some example success criteria and pilot plan documents ready to share with the client. The things that irritate you when procuring technology are likely to be the same things that irritate clients too, so you need to avoid them. Client pilots can be hard to get off the ground. There is an inherent reluctance within law firms to go to a client with something that is less than perfect. Frankly, for the same reasons it is hard to get pilots going in your own firm, it can be hard with your clients – just like your lawyers, your clients will not have a lot of spare time on their hands that they can spend on pilots.

An A-Z of useful (legal and non-legal) methodologies – taking what is useful and applying a liberal dose of common sense

There are many frameworks and methodologies out there for project and innovation management and many different (costly) courses and accreditations – we are probably about to do a disservice to all the highly skilled expert project managers, including the ones we employ, as we rattle through an outline of some of the better-known approaches. Whilst Stuart is a certified Lean Six Sigma Master Black Belt, Catriona is generally just quite well organized, logical, and has adopted bits from various methodologies that seem to make what she needs to do each day work. Who knows if some formal project management training would have improved this? Even if you are an expert in a particular project management methodology, you are unlikely to be able to follow it to the letter in a law firm (especially if working on projects involving more than business services). We are quite content to learn about the various approaches and try them out to see what works in our organization to bring structure to our innovation efforts.

Table 1: Description of project management methodologies

Methodology	Description
Agile	This is a software development technique that breaks down a project into phases, with a focus on ensuring continuous improvement by releasing various versions of software and seeking customer feedback. As an approach, it is more interactive than some traditional models and enables projects to be revised as they develop.
Checklist manifesto	In the book of the same name, Atul Gawande, a surgeon, explains how errors of ineptitude (not making correct use of what we know) are the cause of many failures in the world and can be remedied by checklists that are written down to guide experts through key aspects of procedures in many different professional fields.[12] This certainly appeals to those of use that are planners.
Critical path method	Using this approach, you identify and schedule all of the tasks that are critical for the success of your project. This includes all the related dependencies, but does not really include any slack for problems arising (the related critical chain project management approach rectifies this and builds in buffers). This methodology can be demonstrated in quite a visual way so that you can see the interconnectivity between different collections of tasks.
Design thinking	Design thinking is a human-centered approach to innovation, promoting the exploration of users, problem redefinition, assumption challenging, prototyping, and testing. It is based on solutions rather than problems.

continued on next page

Methodology	Description
Jobs to be done	Jobs to be done advocates a perspective where, rather than think about the customer or the product, you focus on the job that the customer is trying to get done. Whilst products come and go, the job to be done remains relatively stable. This probably appeals to us as it is not that far removed from trying to work out what the problem is you are trying to solve.
Kanban	Kanban is a variation of agile frameworks and involves a visual portrayal of tasks on a virtual board, with columns denoting different stages of a process. Work is moved into the column of the stage it is at, meaning you can spot bottlenecks as you can physically see the contents of a column increase. Our Dev Ops boards work a bit like a Kanban, giving us a high-level overview of the stage a project is at.
Lean	The Lean methodology originated in the Toyota Manufacturing System and is focused on minimizing waste from three causes – wastefulness, unevenness, and overburden.
Lean Six Sigma	A blend of the Lean methodologies and Six Sigma methodologies (that originated out of Motorola). This framework focuses on ensuring consistency of approach by trying to reduce variation and eliminate defects. A define, measure, analyze, improve, control (DMAIC) process is used – similar to Lean's plan, do, check, act.
Legal Design Thinking	Design thinking with "legal" added in front of it to be specialized. Currently on trend.

continued on next page

Methodology	Description
Service Design	This is a process that aims to optimize experiences for customers based on a given context and the service providers. It aims to provide more delightful experiences and looks to ensure the back ends and front ends of systems work well for their respective users and are joined up.
Scrum	Scrum is an agile framework, but it is more prescriptive, with roles such as Scrum Master. Projects are broken down into timed sprints, with an array of meetings as part of each sprint, ranging from a daily stand up to a sprint retrospective. We have always found sprints hard to deliver, despite our best intentions, but on some projects we have effectively used daily stand ups to review progress and eliminate barriers.
Waterfall	This approach sees tasks, as the name suggests, completed in a linear order with one process being completed before another can start. We have not found that this methodology fits our innovation projects where there are usually overlapping phases and not everything can be defined at the beginning.

Example pilot action plan

Document control

Current version:	
Document title:	
Date of publication:	
Document owner:	
Document approver:	
Last review:	
Review schedule:	

Document version control

Version/status	Release description	Date of issue

Background

Before committing to deliver a pilot, we need to complete some planning documents and agree on the success criteria so that:

- We have a clear understanding of what is trying to be achieved;
- We can look at the return on investment and costs associated with continuing with the work;
- We can make the best use of any software during the pilot;
- We can see if there are any similar use cases; and
- We can disseminate the lessons learned.

Use case description:	
Technology to be utilized:	
Subject matter experts:	
Innovation project team:	

Success criteria

Success criteria can include:

- Quicker document review times;
- Improved efficiencies (e.g. priorities review, early identification of key issues, reporting capabilities);
- Reduced cost;
- Enhanced consistency; and
- Scalability.

Please detail the success criteria for this project.

Success criteria	**Agreed**
1.	
2.	
3.	

Key dates

Pre-pilot governance completed	
Assessment criteria agreed	
Documents obtained (if applicable)	
Documents uploaded (if applicable)	
Training completed	
User acceptance testing start (if required)	
User acceptance testing end (if required)	
Pilot start	
Mid-pilot review	
End of pilot	
End of pilot review	

Additional considerations

This can include things like:

- Document removal;
- Folder organization;
- Future release functionality;
- Support desk; and
- Different use cases.

Please detail any additional considerations for this project.

Additional considerations

Actions
1.
2.
3.

Pre-pilot action plan

Task	Action	Details	Notes	Person responsible	Date due	Completed
1. Governance						
1.1	Risk department reviewed and approved terms and conditions?	Yes/No/NA				
1.2	Information Security documentation completed?	Yes/No/NA				
1.3	Information Security documentation signed off by risk department?	Yes/No/NA				
1.4	Is a DPIA required?	Yes/No				
1.5	Is the DPIA completed, including risk department sign off?	Yes/No/NA				

continued on next page

Task	Action	Details	Notes	Person responsible	Date due	Completed
1.6	Is an NDA required?	Yes/No/NA				
1.7	Is the NDA completed and executed?	Yes/No/NA				
1.8	All tasks diarized in dev ops?	Yes/No				
1.9	Is pilot internal or with clients?					
2. Pricing						
2.1	Is internal budget required/ secured?	Yes/No/NA				
2.2	Client contributing?	Yes/No/NA				
3. Client						
3.1	Client consent required?	Yes/No/NA				
3.2	Client consent requested?	Yes/No/NA				
3.3	Client consent agreed?	Yes/No/NA				
4. Success criteria						
4.1	Success criteria drafted?	Yes/No/NA				
4.2	Success criteria agreed?	Yes/No/NA				

continued on next page

Task	Action	Details	Notes	Person responsible	Date due	Completed
5. Training						
5.1	Training participants known?	Yes/No/NA				
5.2	Training arranged?	Yes/No/NA				
5.3	Training completed?	Yes/No/NA				
5.4	How-to guide/standard operating procedure (SOP) required?	Yes/No/NA				
5.5	How-to guide/SOP completed?	Yes/No/NA				
6. Documents (if applicable)						
6.1	Documents obtained?	Yes/No/NA				
6.2	Documents securely stored?	Yes/No/NA				
6.3	Documents decrypted?	Yes/No/NA				
6.4	Documents uploaded?	Yes/No/NA				
7. Systems governance						
7.1	Folder/asset structure?	Yes/No/NA				
7.2	Who needs access (including innovation) and level of permission?					

continued on next page

Task	Action	Details	Notes	Person responsible	Date due	Completed
8. Feedback						
8.1	Feedback mechanism agreed?	Yes/No/NA				
8.2	Feedback interviews required?	Yes/No/NA				
8.3	Feedback interviews scheduled if required?	Yes/No/NA				
8.4	Feedback questionnaire required?	Yes/No/NA				
8.5	Feedback questionnaire drafted if required?	Yes/No/NA				
8.5	Feedback questionnaire agreed if required?	Yes/No/NA				

Chapter checklist

- ☐ How can you collect ideas from your organization and clients?
- ☐ Do you want some quick wins or a big bang?
- ☐ Do you need to be able to prioritize ideas and, if so, how are you going to do it?
- ☐ What processes work in other teams that you can borrow? What do other law firms do?
- ☐ Do you have a high-level pilot process and plan?
- ☐ Do you have a preferred project management approach in your organization?

References

1 Fouzder, M., "Artificial intelligence mimics judicial reasoning", *The Law Society Gazette*, 22 June 2016. See: www.lawgazette.co.uk/law/artificial-intelligence-mimics-judicial-reasoning/5056017.article.

2 See chapter eight for more innovation pitfalls.

3 See chapter seven for more on working with academia.

4 Whittle, S., "Weightmans partners with University of Liverpool and Kira systems to develop AI capable of legal reasoning", 12 June 2018. See: www.weightmans.com/media-centre/news/weightmans-partners-with-university-of-liverpool-and-kira-systems-to-develop-ai-capable-of-legal-reasoning/
"Computer Scientists win 'Best use of Technology' award at Modern Law Awards", 19 February 2019. See: https://news.liverpool.ac.uk/2019/02/19/computer-scientists-win-best-use-of-technology-award-at-modern-law-awards/.

5 See chapter four for more on forming an innovation team.

6 For example, an aggregated summary view of all data on all of the matters on which we are instructed by an individual client.

7 "I didn't spend three years and £60,000 getting a university degree, a year at law college and two years as trainee to be a data entry clerk."

8 Al-Abdulkarim, L., Atkinson, K., Bench-Capon, T., Whittle, S., Williams, R., and Wolfenden, C., "Noise Induced Hearing Loss: An Application of the Angelic Methodology", *Legal Knowledge and Information Systems*, Volume 302, 2017.
Al-Abdulkarim, L., Atkinson, K., Bench-Capon, T., Whittle, S., Williams, R., and Wolfenden, C., "Noise induced hearing loss: Building an application using the ANGELIC methodology", *Argument & Computation*, Volume 10 (1), 2019. See: https://content.iospress.com/articles/argument-and-computation/aac181005.
Atkinson, K., Bench-Capon, T., Routen, T., Sanchez, A., Whittle, S., Williams, R., and Wolfenden, C., "Realising ANGELIC designs using logiak", *Legal Knowledge and Information Systems: JURIX 2019: The Thirty-second Annual Conference*, Volume 322, 2019. See https://livrepository.liverpool.ac.uk/id/eprint/3081251.

9 See bAIley case study in chapter two.

10 "See the possibility", 18 May 2023. See: www.weightmans.com/about-us/see-the-possibility/.

11 Segment heads are responsible for our client-facing work. We have Built Environment, Corporates, Health, Individuals, Insurance, OMB (Owner Managed Businesses), and Public Bodies.

12 Gawande, A., *The Checklist manifesto*, New York: Metropolitan Books, 2009.

Chapter 4:
Skills, team, and bringing others with you – recruiting your "pirates in the navy"

People can make or break an innovation or product initiative – curating an innovation team with a diverse mix of skills is therefore vital to foster successful innovation. It does, however, present some challenges, not least managing such a diverse (and likely more rebellious than is normal in a law firm) bunch of people, and indeed being managed yourself. Unless money and time is not a constraint, when you are setting up an innovation function, you are likely to need to beg and borrow people from other areas of the business.[1] This means you are going to have to try and ensure as good a mix of diverse skills as you can. You are also likely to find yourself often having to learn new things and fill in the gaps – certainly a growth mindset is required! The same applies when you are looking to expand an existing team or department – you have to ensure you do not recruit in your own image; the more unlike you the better your prospects for innovation.

How it helps to be a jack of all trades

Diversity of experience really helps a group to approach a problem from many different angles. This does not just mean a collection of lawyers with different legal specialisms, but a collection of people from around your organization, which could include project managers, business analysts, developers, or campaigns experts. Within these types of roles, you are likely to have a mix of people – some of whom have only worked in professional services and others who have worked in more diverse industries, all of which adds to the diversity of viewpoints. You also want a spread of seniority (provided you have made it a safe space for anyone to contribute, regardless of seniority).

Within lawyers, diversity of experience is key again – this means you do not want two employment lawyers who are only different in the sense that one deals with unfair dismissal claims and the other with claims about wages. You want lawyers who know, or are happy to learn, about a broad spread of the markets in which your organization works, in terms of both clients and legal problems. On reflection, it is probably not a coincidence that the areas of law we practiced (professional indemnity and costs) gave us both a wide experience of seeing many different types of legal work, leading us to know a little about a lot of things (and, usefully, usually different things). The breadth of knowledge, rather than depth specifically, enabled us to think differently about how to approach problems and make connections between different areas of work our organization does, which we doubt would have been the case if we had a narrow sphere of expertise.

How to encourage rebel ideas

Matthew Syed's book[2] is a great manifesto, not only on the need to encourage cognitive diversity, but also on the steps you need to take to get there. Innovation in professional services is a great example where the outcome is usually greater than the sum of its parts.

The way lawyers are trained does not easily lend itself to a cohort of people with rebellious, or indeed always creative, ideas. Whilst lawyers are trained to argue, this is with other lawyers in an underlying framework (the legislation and case law) and, for some, with the rules (the Court process). Whilst as a sweeping generalization they are usually happy to argue with anyone, this argumental approach leads to the best outcomes when the underlying framework is understood (for example, how to write the features and benefits of a product in a way that is compelling to the intended buyer) or the rules (for example, how the technology, scrum, or lean product management works). Whilst the lawyers get used to a different way of thinking, it may be that you need separate workshops in your organization with different groups of people to ensure that you get the most out of them. This can be a challenge when resources are tight, but is usually preferable to having poor levels of engagement in a workshop, or worse still, an echo chamber. There is nothing that will stop the formation of rebellious ideas quicker than an echo chamber and it is a particularly disheartening meeting or workshop to be in. If you know in advance that your participants are at risk of this, then there are some steps you can take to try and minimize it.

Often, some pre-workshop activity can enable a variety of ideas to surface. For example, you could set up an online collaboration board with specific areas for people to add ideas to, vote on suggestions, or answer questions. This needs to be provided with enough time in advance of the session to properly engage with it and with a deadline set for completion. What you are trying to do is to allow enough opportunity for people to express different views, in a less challenging environment, which an asynchronous method of work (such as an online collaboration board) can encourage. This method also means people can share views and ideas anonymously and allows for reflection in advance of the meeting. A more drastic approach may be to ban senior people from the session (or from speaking first) to avoid the highest paid person's opinion (HiPPO) bias.

Intrapreneurship – finding your "pirates in the navy"[3]

Starting a new function or area of work in an existing professional services firm is difficult. We set out in chapter two how we started our innovation part-time around other roles we had within our organization, getting enough interest and success to keep going and scaling incrementally. Realistically, unless your organization has a bottomless pit of money, this is how you are likely to have to start, with small steps and some quick wins to gather momentum within your organization. These early successes were very hard work. In the early days, three of us[4] wore out a lot of shoe leather visiting clients, potential collaborators, and suppliers to discuss innovation with anyone that would listen, and not everyone wanted to listen. We did not always understand the demos we saw and could not always elegantly articulate our solutions but this improved until over time we honed our patter and were using innovation as a way of opening doors to discussions with clients.

This led to us securing budget, both for experimentation and people – we created legal engineer roles and eventually a structure reflecting different levels of experience. The legal engineer role sits at the interface between law, innovation, and other business services teams, often acting as a translator to allow the rapid development of solutions. We also took the opportunity whenever it has arisen to ensure there is a career pathway for progression as a legal engineer, and we now have four levels ranging from junior legal engineer to lead legal engineer – the roles are differentiated by the scale of the projects they are responsible for, their supervision of others, and the depth of their technical expertise. Initially, the people in these roles were internal candidates, which worked well as the innovation team became established as they knew the lay of the land and how to influence the stakeholders in the firm. As the popularity of roles like legal engineers grew, there have been external appointments too, bringing in a wave of new approaches (from their previous work) to problem solving.

The proliferation of new roles, regardless of the specific title, usually resulted in their incumbents doing a number of core things.

1. Finding and collecting ideas from clients and from the business and then attempting to solve them.
2. Finding new technology that could solve existing problems and horizon scanning for what could come next.
3. Understanding, and being able to use and build on, technology used by innovation teams (such as document review, document automation software, and client portals) and building client-facing solutions.
4. Upskilling colleagues and the wider business in all things innovation.
5. Discussing innovation with clients and providing demos and onboarding.
6. Generally experimenting with new technology (for example, large language models).

Some firms aligned legal engineers to specific software or software functionality, such as document review. In that instance, the legal engineer would perform the above tasks with reference to this narrower specialism. Recognizing that being a jack of all trades had worked ok for us, we made a deliberate choice to develop a team of legal engineers who were technology-agnostic and could work across the full range of our stack. Over time, they have of course developed some preferences or deeper expertise regarding particular tools, but everyone has a baseline level of technology knowledge.

The core components of the roles have largely remained the same; however, the time spent on each aspect has evolved as demand for innovation has increased. It got to the stage that focus was spread too thinly as certain activities, such as building client-facing tools, took an increasing amount of time, which then left less time for everything else. As a result, we created the legal technologist role to take on more of the work around upskilling colleagues and discussing innovation with clients, performing demos and onboarding. Although this role was helpful with spreading the internal message and led us to develop our Weightmans Institute for Future Innovation (WIFI) program,[5] the client aspect of the role never really took off as we had hoped and remains a work in progress. It was at this stage we became a product and innovation department, which gave us the chance to review our existing structure and create some new roles.

This led to the establishment of product and innovation partner roles. A product and innovation partner is aligned to six of our seven client-facing segments. Crucially (and deliberately), this is not a full-time role – the product and innovation partners spend 60 percent of their time[6] on product and innovation, with the remaining time for their previous role – which could be legal work, managing client relationships, internal management, or a mixture of all three. The fact that these individuals retain their link to the client and legal work is very important as it allows us to hear client problems firsthand and discuss ideas with clients. In an effort to break down information silos, the product and innovation partners also share this information amongst themselves as a group. This has resulted in opportunities with clients that we do not think would have happened otherwise and we encourage multiple product and innovation partners to be involved in projects where there is crossover with the ultimate market. This helps them to have a level of ownership of the projects and a chance to adapt it, or the marketing of it, to their particular segment. The product and innovation partners sit at the intersection between clients and business services; whilst they have some technological knowledge, they are not expected to be able to code. Rather, their role is to broadly understand the capabilities of the innovation technology and its application to client problems, and to share the problems so that the rest of the product and innovation team can think of potential solutions.

Innovation is contagious

Innovation is all about collaboration and when everything is going well, innovation is contagious; the problem is that when it is not going well, it is also contagious. A lot of innovation is a hard slog, and keeping everyone upbeat can be difficult. In an ideal world, there will always be at least one project that is going well that enables you all to see the glimmer of light and keep going, but in reality, things tend to go wrong on multiple projects at the same time. It can often help to get views on how to solve a particular barrier on a project from members of the team who are not directly working on it, as that distance from the day-to-day issues can sometimes bring much needed perspective. Failing that, the much-quoted aphorism "This too shall pass" comes into play, and it does.

Scaling an innovation team can be tricky; in the early days, it can feel a bit like *The Three Musketeers* as you are a close-knit, nimble group working together and solving clients' problems. While your processes are still evolving and there are only a few of you actively working on innovation, everyone knows everything about all of the projects and you can pick up other projects with ease. Fast forward a couple of years to when the team is bigger, there is increased demand for innovation, and a demonstration of return on investment is required, then there is simply too much going on for everyone to know the ins and outs of all projects. This change, from almost carefree innovation to something with much more governance, can be difficult to adapt to. Even though you are working in a change role, that doesn't mean you are necessarily 100 percent comfortable yourself with all change, and this is entirely normal. As innovation scales, there are likely to be more requirements to demonstrate and document project processes and updates, pilot plans, prioritization matrices, and so on – in short, more managing up. We have found using Azure DevOps to track projects has worked well and it is easy enough to export updates so you can report in whatever way you need to. Despite an increase in innovation governance, you do not want innovation to feel sterile. The focus has to remain on trying new things and approaches rather than the actual outcome – fast failure and all that (although we do prefer fast success as a rule!).

In the early days of forming a team you have two options – play to everyone's strengths or push people in at the deep end. Our foray into innovation meant that both of us were, by necessity, thrown in at the deep end as there was no one else from whom to learn. However, we recognize that this is not always the best way. It normally helps to play to strengths so that people are encouraged and feel that this is a role they can do well in.

Over time, you can encourage people out of their skills comfort zone into learning other skills. We found that a good way for people to learn some of the required skills is:

- Watch another in action;
- Practice with support;
- Perform with a safety net; and
- Practice without support.

As an example, if you have someone junior who has had little client contact, you could start by taking them to client meetings or workshops in a supporting role so that they can see someone who has that skill in action. After the meeting, you will want to debrief with them what they thought went well and what could be improved, and how they may adapt what they saw to their own style. Ideally, you want them to watch a couple of people who are good at the skill to see different approaches. Stage two would have them involved in delivering a part of a meeting or workshop – initially ringfenced in terms of content, so they are not overwhelmed by both learning the content and practicing the skill. You ensure they are practiced so they are comfortable with the content and discuss potential client questions and how comfortable they are with dealing with questions. Stage three sees them supported by an expert acting as a safety net – with them leading an increasing amount of a client meeting or workshop, but with the expert there if they need help. As the expert, you have to be careful not to just wade in and undermine them; you need to wait to be brought into any discussion by them. The final step is when they have practiced sufficiently that they can do the meetings or workshops on their own and then, in turn, take another colleague through this process as they become the one with expertise in the skill. This doesn't then mean you let them loose on all meetings and workshops – if there are ones that are likely to be harder, for example, then you can go back to an earlier stage and double hand.

It is not the size of the innovation team that matters, but the careful curation of it

Variety of skills, rather than size, is the key factor when curating an innovation team. As a caveat, in the beginning the same people are likely to wear multiple hats and, over time, the group is likely to develop new skills. What you need is a good mix! It is also perfectly possible for people to wear different hats in different projects, and perhaps even with different people or stakeholders. Innovation is definitely the place for a growth mindset as, if you happen to be the least-worst person at a skill, then you are going to have to be the one to push through and develop the skill to keep everything moving. Innovation will give you plenty of opportunities to practice a skill and try different approaches and it is worth taking advantage of this. It can also be useful to speak to people within your organization who have the skill, but perhaps in a different context; for example, if you need to upskill on talking to clients then it is worth talking to a lawyer who is good at sales. In this section we cover some of the skills we have found essential to have in the team.

The planners

We love a plan! Planning in the context of innovation may sound counterintuitive – surely innovation occurs when you are experimenting? We have found that whilst with innovation there is a fair element of trial and error and luck, you will want to do this in as much of a systematic way as possible (recognizing the oxymoron) to maximize your chances of success. We are not advocating that everyone involved in innovation needs to have a project management qualification, but a base level of organization is required, not least as there are often multiple projects with competing deadlines to juggle. This means people need to be able to effectively manage their own time and plan out tasks in terms of length of time and priority. Some can manage their own tasks and time effectively just using tools like Outlook or OneNote, and this is fine on an individual level, but not as useful for a team perspective on what is going on. We use Microsoft's Dev Ops (not in the way it intended) to manage all projects and activity, which works well for us as everyone on a project can see what is happening and it can be made quite visual. The fact that all the communication can be done in the software and is linked to each specific item of work means there is no need to search through an email chain to find the pertinent piece of information.

Planning in an innovation context can take many forms and we have found planning to be particularly useful for premortems and skills expansion.

- *Premortems* – without even really realizing it, as we start to plan a new project (whether piloting a particular technology or building a software solution for a client's problem), we have unwittingly usually carried out a premortem exercise, even if not labelled as such. We assume a project has gone wrong before it has started, and the premortem usually takes the form of a collective brain dump of all the potential ways that the project may fail, informed by lessons learnt on previous projects if applicable. Whilst this might sound like a pessimistic mindset in which to start a project, it allows us to consider and mitigate potential hurdles early on, so that a problem is not a surprise if it does arise and we already have spent some time on a potential solution. It also allows us to reflect on previous projects and acknowledge what has gone well that can be reused in the new context. For example, it may be that a particular format and cadence of communication worked well with a similar group of people. It acts as an upfront acknowledgment that innovation is hard and many projects won't go to plan or indeed even succeed. Rather than being overly pessimistic, premortems allow an open discussion of potential failure points, with the safety net of them not having occurred and without any fear of being impolitic – as opposed to a postmortem where, even with the best of intentions, it can be hard to prevent it being an unhelpful blame game. The plan can then be reviewed and strengthened in light of the premortem. It also acts as a high-level notice of things to look out for during the lifecycle of the project, which may affect the outcome, reducing the risk of not spotting the warning signs. It also provides the language to facilitate that discussion if required, as it can be linked to the earlier discussions.

- *Skills expansion: new skills, more mastery* – although as an innovation team you are constantly learning, this is often in a technical area of expertise or a project planning and delivery context. As your innovation efforts expand, you will be looking to ensure that you have a good mix of technical expertise, and at a variety of levels of mastery. Whilst you want everyone in a team to have a basic level of mastery of all the technology you work on, most people will demonstrate a preference for a particular technology, area of law, or stage of a project. To avoid key person dependency, it is useful to plan how this expertise will be shared and how others can be upskilled. It is important not to overlook the more interpersonal skills such as effective communication, building rapport, persuasion, and the people side of change management. Despite working in a world of change, it doesn't necessarily mean those working in innovation like change when done to them any more than the rest of the population, certainly in our experience! It is therefore important to ensure training focuses on developing and honing a wide variety of interpersonal skills, with plenty of opportunity to then put this into practice. We have found Team Canvas,[7] sales training, and LinkedIn training sessions to be good mediums to help people develop and refine these skills.

The thinkers

Often closely linked with planners, thinkers are an important group to have in the team. Whilst some people struggle with the lack of structure often found in the day-to-day workings of an innovation team, the thinker uses this to their advantage, happy to ruminate on a particular problem, or to generally research and explore an area. They may have a particular interest in problem solving or strategy and harnessing this can be useful in developing the overall team's skills and strategies. Innovation teams need the space, both collectively and individually, to think, as well as a suitable forum to exchange ideas and discuss topics. It is easy to fall into the trap of assuming a meeting where you ask for input is sufficient. However, this does not take into account different preferences, which may include exchanging ideas or views asynchronously instead of, prior to, or after a meeting. This asynchronous exchange may take place via an online collaboration space to record views (even anonymously if required) or maybe via virtual polls to gauge the mood of a group about a workshop. Thinkers are particularly helpful in premortem discussions, especially if they know all possible causes of failure are available to be explored.

It is important to encourage thinkers not to focus on one particular thing in minute detail – you want broad thinking, not overthinking, and an ability to multitask remains important. There may be a tendency to veer into topics the thinker is comfortable with, rather than looking at new areas, and this may become apparent around topics such as commercialization, or if a quick decision is needed. You don't want the thinkers so caught up in thinking that they can never act on gut instinct. There is always more than one way to solve a problem and encouraging thinkers to make decisions in a specific time frame or without every single piece of information can help ensure they do not inadvertently delay or impact a project.

The doers

A team of just planners and thinkers could quickly lead to inertia if none of the many well-planned ideas are ever actioned. As much as we like a plan and time to think, you have to make sure you don't get stuck in planning and thinking paralysis so that nothing ever gets done. By its very nature, innovation is experimental, and you are not going to be able to cover all ideas and plans before you start. Indeed, as you progress through a project you may have to change course. It is always helpful to have a fair proportion of people in a team who are happy getting involved in action, especially when things may not be as crystalized as you would like. Often the "doing" is part and parcel of learning and problem solving.

What usually identifiers a doer is that when you get new technology to pilot or use, they are the first to try it, even before any training is provided. They are often self-taught technologists who are good at figuring out how things work and how to join up pieces of technology. It is still worth getting them trained if the provider offers courses to ensure nothing obvious is overlooked in their haste to start, or you may end up creating problems in future by doing something in a way that the technology supplier may not consider best practice.

The challenge with doers is making sure they can bring the rest of the team along with them on a project so that others still feel able to make suggestions. You do not want the doers so far ahead that nobody else gets a chance to feed into project decisions, or that you collectively assume that the only way to solve the problem is the way in which the doer has started. Sometimes, it will be necessary to ask for others to suggest different ways of solving the same problem in order to achieve this, perhaps giving your thinkers some dedicated time to work on the problem and share their views.

The risk takers

Innovation teams seem to attract people with a higher propensity to take risk (in a professional services context) than you would expect, just given the nature of the work. Many, like us, may have started in an innovation role when it was nascent in their organization, leaving a role that they knew inside out to try something different with the inherent risk that it could all fail. We initially recruited our innovation team from internal candidates and needed people brave enough to buy into the vision and willing to give it a go. That said, even with a group of risk takers, there are still levels of risk; you do not want people who are undisciplined with security or data, for example. What you do need is people happy to take a gamble on a project or an idea – so you want people who can take a punt effectively (appreciating that no one is ever going to get it 100 percent perfect).

Ideally, even within a group of known risk takers, you want a variety of acceptance of different levels of risk, or risk in different contexts. There may be times where, as a group, you would like to work to a different level of risk than your wider organization may be happy to accept. It is possible to shift an organization's risk appetite, but expect to have many conversations with stakeholders, often on a loop and be prepared to show your reasoning and steps taken to mitigate risk. As you may expect, it is easier to shift an organization's risk appetite if you can get your risk and compliance team on board. There will be some situations where, as an innovation team, you adopt a cautious approach to a particular risk, and it is useful to know what these situations are in advance and for you to pick your battles. For example, suppliers who host in a particular country may be off-limits in your organization and you are unlikely to be able to change that, so better to focus your efforts elsewhere. In scenarios where a range of risk appetite is acceptable, it can be helpful when attempting to make a decision to discount both extremes on the risk continuum (i.e., the very high risk and very low risk option) and work on forming a consensus from here.

The rebels

We would probably consider ourselves relatively comfortable in challenging the status quo or even being what might otherwise be considered as rebellious. This desire to push boundaries or challenge accepted ways of thinking is certainly a trait that people who work in innovation often possess. Can you imagine trying to have to manage us! It is a quality that can be particularly useful if you just need to get things done and cut through bureaucracy. Professional services organizations can sometimes end up severely hampered by bureaucracy, with a large number to be informed and consulted on any project, a lack of actual decisions, and scopes extended to an unmanageable size. Whilst there are often valid reasons for this, it can slow down the pace and energy required on an innovation project quite considerably.

Of course, even in an innovation context, you need some way of running projects and prioritizing them – we are not advocating for a Wild West where anything goes. However, there are occasions where cutting through the bureaucracy is called for. There is no hard and fast rule for identifying when this is the case – a lot of this is intuition and knowing your own organization. One of us has been prepared to concede that, on occasion, it is better to ask for forgiveness rather than permission; the other can attest that this should be used sparingly!

It can be hard, as you become more successful in your innovation efforts, to not curtail this rebellious quality in your growing team as it is often where many of the lightbulb moments occur. With bigger teams and more projects inevitably comes more structure and governance, but you need to work hard to ensure this is proportionate and does not stifle behaviors that are otherwise very useful in an innovation team. You may find that your role shifts as you become more senior away from rebellion as you are more alive to the politicking required in larger organizations. You may find yourself in more of a cheerleading role, supporting your innovation colleagues to find their cause and develop their own rebellious streak; after all, no one likes a rebel without a cause.

The big-picture people

You will usually have multiple projects running at any one time within the team or department – at the same time as working in an ever-changing technological landscape and trying to support your organization with a balanced portfolio of projects (with a strategic thread running through them). As a result, it can be hard to see the wood for the trees and you want someone who can stand back and work out how it all joins up, from several angles:

- *Internally:* how do projects link between various departments?
- *Clients:* which clients, regardless of how you segment them, are having similar problems?
- *Systems and technology:* where can you pass information? How does it all connect to internal or client core systems? How do you keep the technology stack current?

Big-picture people are good at finding a core theme or thread in a collection of ideas and seeing how they fit into an ever-changing horizon. Sometimes, this is a bit easier if you are more detached from the specifics of individual projects.

The details people

One of your authors is happiest in the weeds and details are their happy place. Provided it is not taken to the extreme of preventing completion, then a healthy interest in details is a skill that collectively benefits an innovation team. It allows you to dot all the Is and cross all the Ts on a project, idea, hypothesis, or piece of research. When you are forming project teams it is useful to have a broad spread of thought and skills, but especially details people to counterbalance some of the other attributes covered here.

The people people

We maintain (including throughout this book) that innovation in a professional services firm is all about the people. However, that does not necessarily mean that you have to be a people person to be successful in innovation; it just means that if you are capable of dealing with a wide variety of people, or indeed tolerate it the best, then you will be the one propelled to keep doing it. This can be exhausting if it is not your natural skill set, but there are often occasions where you have to wear multiple hats, and this is just one of them. Dealing well with different groups of people and audiences is certainly a skill that gets better with practice, and it should not be only the people people who are pushed to deal with people. Tailoring your communication style to different audiences, selling the innovation story, listening well, and building empathy are such crucial skills for innovation that even the unwilling need to be encouraged to practice and expand their skill set.

Chapter checklist

- ☐ Do you know your skill set and do you have a growth mindset?
- ☐ How can you best bring together groups of people with cognitive diversity?
- ☐ Where can you find your pirates in the navy – are they hidden in plain sight?
- ☐ What job descriptions and titles do you need?
- ☐ Have you got a mixed skill set in the innovation team? How can this be encouraged?

References

1 See chapter two for how we got started.
2 Syed, M., *The Power of Diverse Thinking. Rebel Ideas*, London: John Murray Publishers Ltd, 2019.
3 See this excellent book – Viki, T., *Pirates In The Navy: How Innovators Lead Transformation*, London: Unbound, 2020.
4 This book's authors and Rob Williams, a Board member and insurance partner by background.
5 See chapter 12 for more on this.
6 Accepting that this is not an exact science – how the 60 percent time commitment is achieved varies depending on the product and innovation partner in question; some like to try and carve out full days, others a proportion each day. There will be weeks when the balance may be a bit off but it tends to even out.
7 See: https://theteamcanvas.com/.

Chapter 5:
When it works – lessons learned

Largely through a process of trial and error, and then by repeating what has worked, we have been able to boil down some of the factors that have made our innovation projects successful.

Not all subject matter experts are born equal – how to spot the right ones

As mentioned before, in law firms, we are not innovating in a vacuum. Our clients have real problems that they are not able to solve for themselves. By definition, if they were able to solve the issue themselves, they would not need to seek help from their suppliers, such as their law firms. It is not universally true, but organizations working in the same or related sectors frequently face the same sort of challenges. However, we also have experience of seemingly very similar businesses, operating in the same sector, who have diametrically opposed reactions to the same potential solution. One will see it as borderline revolutionary for them, the other is not very impressed. Some of the challenges that organizations face can be caused by changes in the law. Examples of this include the shortage of lorry drivers in the UK in 2021 and the impact on holiday pay calculations following the Supreme Court's decision of *Harpur Trust v. Brazel* (2022) UKSC 21. This plays well into involving law firms in creating solutions as the starting point is to understand the differing effects of any changes in the law in different industries. If you think about those sorts of factors, this is where you can start to find the sort of subject matter expert that you will need.

It is overused, but your perfect subject matter expert will have a real passion for their area of law or practice, their clients, and the sectors in which their clients operate. Again, it is trite, but they will also tend to be intrinsically curious. Curious about their clients and how they work, curious about the sectors in which their clients operate, curious about technology. They are not the sort of people who will start with a solution but by trying to properly understand the problem they are trying to solve. They will tend to have a deep understanding of the clients who they work for. They won't be the sort of lawyer of whom a client's in house general counsel will recite the oft-repeated homily that *"Our lawyers don't understand our business"*. They are intrinsically interested in the sectors in which their clients operate. They expose themselves to their clients' wider sectors and issues and consequently will be the sort of person that willingly (i.e., does not have to be nagged or brow beaten into so doing) posts or writes posts, blogs, or articles on subjects of interest to their clients. They will tend to have an extensive network both externally and internally, which are both a cause and a consequence of their inherent interest in their area and their clients' sectors. They will be engaged with their clients so they know how they operate, the lingo, and the operational details of their clients' industries. By analogy to the legal industry, we do not want to have to explain to a supplier how a law firm works (such as what a billable hour is) and, in a similar way, clients do not want to have to explain the nuances of their market.

One thing they do not need is to be able to write computer code, but they will be the sort of person who knows their way around Word styles and have a more than passing acquaintance with Excel (a much-underrated tool in law firms). They may not be software experts, but they have an appreciation of the sorts of capabilities of these solutions. They are the sort of person whose first thought is, *"Is there a better or easier way of doing this?"* and then use their initiative to either find someone who might be able to help them or perform their own research, appreciating that they are not likely to be the first person ever to think that there must be an easier way of taking a long list of items and summarizing how many of each item there is (pivot table, anyone?). They will tend to be, almost by definition, people who you would describe as self-starters; people with drive who see problems as potential opportunities.

Their ideas can come from changes in the law, or from novel applications of existing law, perhaps to help organizations navigate regulatory environments. The ideas can be purely technology based, but more often than not are a combination of technology and services (at some level most innovation in law firms fall into this category). Inevitably there is an element of serendipity to all of this, but these people maximize their chances of serendipity by making sure they are talking to their clients and colleagues. Internal networking features at this point – they are likely to be people who might be able to help or who might have come across something similar in their particular niche. It also helps cross-fertilize ideas that work in one area of the firm for certain clients and in turn to realize that others in the firm have clients that face similar challenges. However benign your firm may be, that internal network is similarly important to enable you to navigate the internal politics of the firm so that, in the words of Stephen Allen, "*You can get shit done*".

This comes back to networking and the fact that these people tend to have effective internal and external networks. They talk to clients – different clients and potential clients. They talk to people in different parts of their clients' organizations as the view from the top can be very different from the view on the ground and the strategic concerns very different from the daily challenges. They also talk to people within their own law firm. They talk to lawyers who act for clients they do not, they talk to lawyers who are in different sectors and who have different specialisms. As we may have mentioned before, lawyers have a very clear ontological view of the world in that it is very neatly divided in to two parts; lawyers and then everyone else. That's not how these people work; they talk to business services people because they understand how sales and marketing people might help them; they talk to people in the IT teams and in the innovation teams and they make use of expertise they do not have to help them explore their ideas. They recognize that whilst they might have a bright idea, they need help in turning that idea in to something concrete. They recognize that whilst they have a deep understanding of their legal specialism, they do not have the deep understanding that someone who has worked in sales for 20 years has and they listen and they take advice on how to go to market, and how to approach clients.

They are collaborative by instinct and recognize that their organization has resources that can help and advise how to turn their idea in to something that will solve a client's problem. They are tenacious. They do not give up when they have to put a business case together and they have another go if the Board is not buying their first business case. They know that just because they have an idea that to them might be the greatest in the world, if no one's buying it, who cares? They are resilient enough to take that on the chin and they are willing to pivot based on some of the things they are learning when they talk to people, both internally and externally. They are comfortable talking to clients when they do not know the answers and are comfortable in not having to supply the answers but to solicit clients' help to collaborate and work out the answers together. They are intrinsically motivated. They are not the sort of person who thinks their job is to throw the idea over the wall for "innovation" to pick it up and run with it. They realize there is not a magic innovation or technology wand that can instantly transform their idea into a beautifully formed perfect solution. Your dream subject matter expert is one who understands their clients so well that they can offer solutions to clients for problems the client may not even have known they had or solutions that the clients would never have contemplated asking for.

An example

One of our clients was a large national employer with many locally managed branches. Occasionally, local managers would be asked to manage an employee to whom the provisions of the Equality Act 2010 applied. Ensuring that the employee is treated fairly, both procedurally and substantively, is a quite detailed process and, as issues related to the Act did not arise very often, the local managers did not have a lot of experience with managing such issues. When issues did arise, that lack of experience led to mistakes, which in turn led to claims under the Act, which tended to be expensive for the organization to deal with. It was never going to be economical for solicitors to advise on each separate employment issue that touched on the Act. Instead, we created an app that would lead managers through the relevant requirements so they could ensure they were treating their employees fairly, which reduced the volume of claims arising. The client would never have asked us to create an app to help with their problem of claims arising out of the inaccurate application of the Act's provisions, so it is the perfect example of a subject matter expert who understood the client's challenges, the law, and the firm's capabilities sufficiently to explore an idea about how to make it easier for the local managers to be procedurally and substantively fair to their employees. It remains a good example of where technology can help by virtue of what it is good at doing, which is repeatable and predictable tasks at scale for low cost. In this case, the client had the confidence that the app had been designed by expert employment lawyers who, in addition to understanding the law, understood the client's operations, enabling us to configure the app to work with the client's existing HR processes.

The ideal subject matter expert knows it takes a lot of hard work and time to talk to clients about their problems and the ideas they might have for solving them in such a way that when the client is ready to buy it is that person to whom they reach out.

Whilst their objectives (in a formal HR sense) don't necessarily have to be aligned to innovation – their motive is to solve clients' problems rather than achieve their objectives – when it comes to prioritization, it clearly helps when the individual's reward is aligned to the innovation projects they are wanting to lead. Particularly where there are revenue targets to achieve off the back of the innovation. That concentrates the mind.

Clearly, to an extent we have described a unicorn. Very few people in any law firm will meet all of these criteria, which is why you need to get the right people together to get the right mix of skills to solve the clients' problems and to turn ideas and opportunities into products and services that can meet specific needs of clients and sectors.

Ensuring you have the right people, in the right room, at the right time, on the right page

In the context of a subject matter expert who may not have all of our requisite qualities, but who has the germ of an idea and a solution that they want to happen but no guidance for how to make it happen, then that is the opportunity for the innovation team to step in. Start by talking to the subject matter expert and getting more detail about the nature of the problem they are trying to solve and explore the potential solution(s) they have in mind. Be prepared for a circular and tortuous conversation – send your most patient colleague in! You will likely need to take them back to get to the nub of the problem that they are trying to solve, and you may sound like a broken record. One of our observations is that where subject matter experts have a deep domain knowledge, the solutions that they identify are necessarily limited by their experience. For example, if they have never come across decision engines or document automation technology, then they are unlikely to suggest those as potential solutions rather than an army of paralegals churning out standard template documents. Concentrating on the problem that you are trying to solve will start to tell you about the skills and backgrounds of the team you need to assemble to turn the idea into something that can be realized. Despite the fact that we have a means of communication over long distances, this sort of discussion is far more effective if it is done in person around a wall of Magic Paper armed with some Post-It notes and an armful of Sharpies.

We mentioned in chapter two the idea one of our subject matter experts had to help organizations struggling to recruit overseas workers through a novel application of immigration law, which another subject matter expert thought clients in the logistics sector could benefit from. Together they had the germ of an idea and, most helpfully, a client that was interested in exploring it. The opportunity to execute was relatively short, not least because it was not beyond any other similarly interested immigration lawyer to work out. The subject matter experts leapt to a solution that involved a small army of paralegals to deliver the service and there then ensued a lengthy email exchange which, by the time it had finished, had involved the managing partner, two Board members, and various other members of the senior leadership team.

With a bit of exploration, and a healthy skepticism that the solution involved an army of paralegals (which we did not have to spare), we identified a group of people to get together in a room. We had the immigration lawyer who had identified the novel application of existing immigration law (we told you lawyers innovate in their core competency at the start of this book). We had the client-relationship partner who understood the logistics sector and who had a client interested in the idea. We had the Board member and department head who would be responsible for resourcing the solution, a couple of legal engineers with deep domain knowledge of a number of our technology solutions we had anticipated might be helpful, and a member of our workflow team as, again, we anticipated that a workflow might need developing to manage the work coming in.

In the space of five or six hours, we started by making sure everyone was on the same page in terms of the problem, which is a non-trivial exercise since, as we all know, the problem with communication is the illusion that it has taken place. We then went through numerous iterations of ideas and solutions until, in a genuine flash of inspiration, one of our group asked the key question that enabled the group to realize that we could automate the solution in a client-facing app. Within two weeks of the meeting, we had a minimum viable product (MVP) that we took to the client who used it successfully. What made the process successful, ultimately, was that the two subject matter experts who were driving the solution were hugely client-focused, which meant they saw the value in giving their time to collaboration with our legal engineers and our workflow developers to rapidly develop a costed, scalable, solution for the client.

Urgent document review

Challenge/opportunity

A commercial client was faced with the prospect of manually reviewing 1,800 documents to respond to a regulatory issue within a restrictive deadline. This piece of work was priced on the basis of requiring a significant number of lawyers to review the documents and manually collate the required information onto a spreadsheet, which was prohibitively expensive for the client. Reducing the volume of documents reviewed would reduce the price, but from a risk perspective would not offer the client the sample size they needed to be representative of their portfolio. As an alternative to a lengthy process of manual sifting, we suggested using an AI-based system to speed up the review and extraction process.

Strategy

The system can find and extract information from unstructured data and documents, and the machine-learning technology can be trained to automatically identify and extract any user-specified information.

We undertook some bespoke training ourselves on a sample of the documents to be able to identify the relevant information. We were also able to utilize some of the pre-existing models which, along with the bespoke training, enabled the system to identify the required information in the remaining documents and allow the team to review them.

People

We had to train people who had never used the system before. This was before the COVID-19 pandemic when online training wasn't really a thing. In total, we trained 20 people virtually across multiple offices. We divided the users into small groups based on their proficiency with the system, which covered people who were new to it, those who needed a refresher, and experts who could be trained on some of the more complex functionality. Those who were initially skeptical and not as keen became keener when they knew it was a way of getting the work done during office hours!

We created a Standard Operating Procedure and a data dictionary, which was circulated to the users, so they had something to use as a reference manual. The raw data that was extracted from the system into a spreadsheet was invaluable in enabling us to reconcile the data into the client's spreadsheet. Dashboard functionality in the system allowed us to allocate work effectively, keeping a track of the volume of documents and progress in reviewing them.

Execution

The process was not just about reading the documents on the system (otherwise you have just chucked technology at the problem and created faster chaos!). The plan comprised:

- Step one: Scope and price project.
- Step two: Define data fields and train lawyers on the software and data fields.
- Step three: Request required documents.
- Step four: Upload documents onto a sharing platform – log on the file tracker and deal with missing documents.
- Step five: Upload documents to the system.
- Step six: Review the documents.
- Step seven: Extract data from the system.
- Step eight: Populate and reconcile client spreadsheet with system data.
- Step nine: Final supervision, reconciliation, and sign off.

Outcome

Compared to a sample reviewed manually, which would have taken upwards of an hour, using the system reduced the review and information extraction to five minutes on average. This enabled us to deliver the project to the client against tight timescales and to review all the documents the client required for less than half the price of reviewing them all manually. We were also able to take on additional work from another firm, which was assisting on the same task but was doing them manually and was not able to get through the volume needed quickly enough to meet the client's deadline.

As our sample was going to be extrapolated across a large set of data, accuracy was critical. The client performed a manual spot check and reported that less than two percent of the data provided was flagged for further analysis by its data verification process (significantly lower than other firms who had performed the same exercise) and this represented just a handful of data points from the original pool of 1,800 documents with tens of thousands of data points.

What did we learn?

- *It is possible to train people at speed to use a new system.* You can train people on new technology and get them going in a morning, but you need to have a strong process for training in advance. This needs to cover the core information that you need for groups of users based on either their experience with the software or the task they will be doing (or both) and team members must be available to deal with any queries as people start using the software.
- *The right people need to read the right part of a document.* When undertaking large document review exercises it can often be helpful to divide the work by data field rather than by document. This means the experienced lawyers can look at the complex provisions and everyone else can help with the more straightforward data.
- *You need a process for supervision and internal audit.* Depending upon the system that you are using this could be using flags, tags, and sampling the exported reports. Whatever you do, you need to devise a clear system and make sure this is understood by the users. For example, you may use flags where someone is not sure that the information is correct and wants a second look, and tags with an agreed escalation structure (e.g. "supervision required").
- *Do not overlook setting up a data dictionary.* As you add more people to document review, it is even more important to have an agreed data dictionary, such as the example below.

Table 1: Data dictionary example.

Software field	Details (including any warnings/ tips)	Complete details in summary field in software? (Yes/No)	Output required for spreadsheet
[Name of system field]	[e.g. "this field has been trained on X type of document so will need a careful review" or "this field will always need supervision check if completed"]	[Do you want people to summarize the clause (if so how), or score according to a numerical or RAG based system, which you need to define]	[Details on format – no £ sign or two decimal places. Details on where this fits in a client's spreadsheet if they have provided one]

- *Be clear on pricing.* Alongside the pricing is it useful to have a scoping document that covers things like the volume of documents, the number of data points (and a definition), and the format of the data required by the client (for example, if they want a date in DD/MM/YYYY format). If the pricing is based on any specific assumptions this should also be clearly specified. This could include things like the provision of documents by a certain date, that there is one document to be reviewed per matter, or that this is purely a data exercise and the client has not asked for advice on any legal, competition, or regulatory issues (or whatever else may be relevant). Work out if you need to factor in preparatory steps (such as obtaining the documents in the first place), dealing with the exported data, and any reconciliation.
- *Work out what your unique document identifier is going to be at the start and communicate it.* You are likely to have several options such as company number, title number, etc. To prevent chaos, you need to stick to it.
- *If this is the first time you have undertaken a particular volume use case, backfill and write a SOP at the conclusion of it.* Your future self will thank you. The SOP should cover things such as:
    - People and roles.
    - Pricing. It is worth making a pricing calculator, if you can, from timings, the number of people, and the administrative support required. Detail in the SOP what it does not include, such as training, or data export and reconciliation. List the factors that would increase or decrease pricing, such as urgency, a high proportion of topics, more than the average number of documents, many untrained software fields, and a high number of system fields. All of this serves as a useful reminder next time you have to deliver a similar project.
    - A process flow, including actions required, outputs, any prerequisites, the person responsible, and people involved.

How to help your subject matter expert with innovation

This is an education piece, which you will need to approach from different angles. The first thing to hold in your head is that the fundamental job of a lawyer is to be right when you advise your clients and identify solutions for clients. But as with all of us, the solutions we are capable of identifying are limited by our own experience and the sorts of things we know. In the immigration example above, our subject matter experts' solution was a service provided by an army of paralegals. A large part of that was a result of their 20 or so years' experience in a law firm where the sorts of solutions provided to clients were fundamentally delivered through people power.

Our experience is that the education needs to be felt and experienced. To that end, the education almost has to be done one subject matter expert at a time. Often the hardest part is to get over the initial skepticism that an innovation team might have something to offer at all. Once this hurdle has been overcome, you can lead the subject matter expert through a conversation so that you can get to a clear definition of the problem that you are trying to solve, as opposed to the subject matter expert's view that your role is simply to deliver the solution that they are suggesting.

If you have had successes in the past with other subject matter experts and delivered something of value, then they can be helpful by sharing their story that, despite their skepticism, they went with the flow and they ended up with something better than they had anticipated. Particularly if that expert has similar experience to the skeptic – seeing something "real" that relates specifically to their own area of interest or expertise can really help. Our experience suggests that, seeing the technology applied to their specific domain and legal specialism is what makes the difference, even when, conceptually, the solution is doing the same thing in a different legal domain is what makes the difference. To a real estate lawyer, simply because a system can extract change of control and jurisdiction clauses from contracts does not mean it can extract rent review clauses and notice provisions from leases, even though, conceptually from the point of view of the system, it is the same problem. You can also elicit support from the manager of the department or team where you had the success as, hopefully, they are already aware of the capabilities of the innovation team and, again, can encourage the skeptic.

In our example above, we had support from the subject matter experts' line managers who, in effect, had asked the innovation team (amongst others) to help take the idea and deliver something that the client-relationship partner could take to her client in a short period of time. The managers helped to explain that if the subject matter experts wanted something delivered quickly, they needed to be part of that process and attend the in-person meeting, which (with a little resistance) they did.

We have run workshops and roadshow demos in the past with varying degrees of success. Part of the challenge with workshops is that they require time from your lawyers – the one thing that they are not blessed with a surfeit of. The people who see the value in such workshops are often not the people who you really need to educate. However, the biggest challenge with workshops is that, however well you structure them, they tend to be too abstract. Which comes back to our original point that, education is most effectively done subject matter expert by subject matter expert, where they can work on an actual solution to an actual problem. This is, however, really time consuming.

One of our subject matter experts had an idea years in the making. We have always had to supply a number of our institutional clients with data that we describe as management information – that is to say, discrete data about the matters we were handling for them. Metadata about matters if you like. This was, and is particularly, the case where we handle portfolios of matters for single clients. For example, we might hold data about a retail client's property estate (such as when the lease is due for renewal, particular restrictions, rental value and so on) or for litigated personal injury claims we might hold the date of the accident, the nature of the injury, whether liability was in dispute and so on. Clients use this data to get high-level views on the portfolio of claims that we handle for them, in some cases to ensure we are complying with service-level agreements (SLAs), and to compare us to their other panel solicitors. Over the more than 20 years we have been doing this (in the early 1990s we created a database for a particular client, which was the genesis of this approach), we have evolved how we present this data to clients. In particular, what started off as spreadsheets with rows and rows of data we have turned into data visualization solutions – off the back of which clients can take action.

Putting this in context, we should say that the collection of this data has always been a challenge. Case handlers do not like doing it and it needs constant attention to make sure the data is complete and correct. Generally, we have limited ourselves to only collecting the specific data that clients have required from us (though our data professionals would like us to collect more, and more granular, data).

In the context of claims arising out of accidents that cause catastrophic injuries, one of our partners had a vision that we could distinguish ourselves in a competitive market by collecting vast volumes of data about these claims (far more data than our clients were asking us to collect) with a view that we might be able to do something with it all to provide additional insights.. There were many hurdles to overcome, including securing client consent, getting to a point where we had sufficient data to be useful (these sorts of claims tend to take a long time to conclude), and actually getting case handlers to complete data fields where the benefit was some time off being realized.

In an example of serendipity, at or around the point that the partner thought there was sufficient data and was talking to the interested market, the legal industry suddenly started looking at innovation and, jumping on that bandwagon, we hired our first data scientists. The partner was then able to join all of the pieces together. We used the data to create models for catastrophic loss claims that helped case handlers reserve[1] more accurately at the outset of claims when they tended to have incomplete information. We were able to show that, where clients had let us use the model on their claims, we could reduce their indemnity spend and claims lifecycle compared to clients who did not. We now market that solution as PREDiCT Large Loss[2] and have extended the concept to lower value claims.

So we had a subject matter expert who understood his market, had a vision, resiliently pursued that vision (against a fair bit of internal skepticism), and made use of expertise around the firm to turn that vision into a solution for which clients were prepared to pay. Almost our archetypal best-case scenario.

Case study – GDPR

Challenge/opportunity

A commercial client was faced with several hundred agreements to review for GDPR points in order to find certain information that would result in an addendum agreement being required. This piece of work was priced on the basis of requiring several weeks onsite with the client, manually reviewing the documents, and collating the required information. As an alternative to a lengthy process of manual sifting, we offered to use an AI-based system, to speed up the review and extraction process.

Strategy

The system can find and extract information from unstructured information and documents, and the machine-learning technology can be trained to automatically identify and extract any user specified information. We undertook some bespoke training on a sample of the documents to be able to identify the relevant information. Once we had trained the system, it was then able to identify the required information in the remaining contracts and allow the team to review them. The dashboard functionality allowed us to allocate work effectively, keeping a track on the volume of unreviewed contracts.

People

This was the first time we used the system on a project for a client and we were lucky in that we worked with a couple of lawyers who were technologically minded and knew it would be better to put some upfront time into training the system rather than going through a pile of documents manually. They were also happy to advocate this approach to the client, and crucially involve the innovation team in those conversations. We were able to speak with the head of legal at the client and demo the system with some sample documents and then answer their questions around information security and how the system worked.

We provided system training on some sample documents for the lawyers, and then assisted them with training and refining the training on their documents.

Execution

Against a tight client deadline and with only a handful of lawyers, we were able to review all the contracts required by the client in their given timescale.

Outcome

Compared to a sample reviewed manually, using the system resulted in a 65 percent reduction in time for the review and information extraction and allowed us to deliver the project to the client against tight timescales. It also allowed us to respond to dynamic, ever-changing data points. The data required by the client changed part-way through the project and, had this been a traditional manual review, all the contracts would have had to have been looked at again from scratch. The system allowed us to deal effectively with this; as extra information was requested we trained on the extra provisions, which could then be applied across all of the contracts that had already been reviewed.

What did we learn?

- *You cannot offer too much support.* We were lucky in this case as our lawyers were technologically minded but, even then, being present to help with document uploads, setting up the file structure, and talk through the best way to set up a worksheet certainly helped. We also assisted with training the model and with the data export. It was not that our lawyers could not have figured it out for themselves, more that it saved them some effort and made the whole process seem very smooth and straightforward.

- *Having the innovation team in client conversations helps.* Speaking to clients directly prevents the backwards and forwards of information exchange, tends to speed the process up, and can stop things being lost in translation (do not underestimate the problems this can cause). It also sends the message to the client that they are important and that you are really joined up on this and so will be easy to do business with.
- *Client FAQ documents help clients have the conversations they need and help you scale.* Often there will need to be further discussions by the client with their colleagues. We have created short FAQ documents for clients to use internally, which explain the problem the technology is solving and that it is augmentation of a lawyer's expertise rather than a replacement of it. It also covers any data or more technical commonly asked questions.
- *You need a system when using technology.* There is no getting around the (frankly boring) aspects of setting up projects, such as a folder structure, a naming convention, how you are going to allocate documents, and what each data field means. In your haste to get started, don't forget this. If you do, throwing technology alone at the problem will simply cause faster and more efficient chaos.

How your subject matter expert should help you

The three crucial things you need from your subject matter expert is their time, an open mind, and a client who has a level of interest – but most importantly they should be willing to invest some of their time with you, even if it is just providing feedback on your ideas. There is also an element of being willing to submit themselves to the process of innovation and product development (the former blurs into the latter).

Every organization has a finite amount of resource available to them. This means that there will always be internal competition for that resource and ultimately means prioritization is necessary. The political landscape in law firms can be particularly challenging when prioritizing resource allocation as every partner, client, practice area, and team will have different things they want to do that requires resource, and often the same pool of resources at the same time. Prioritizing one partner, department, or team over another can require the judgment of Solomon. One approach is to allocate a little time to every possible demand to try and keep everyone happy, but this means everything takes such a long time that all you end up doing is keeping everyone at an equal level of unhappiness. No one gets what they want when they want it, but at least there is no jealousy as no one sees anyone else getting what they want instead.[3] Strategically, the latter is unsustainable but securing resource allocation is an area where your subject matter expert can help. The enthusiasm of your subject matter expert can (with your help) persuade the business that their project is the one to which resource should be allocated by submitting a business case for investment.

All of the factors that make for a good subject matter expert also make up the areas in which they can help with the project altogether. Their external networking means they can talk to multiple clients and ascertain whether the issue is that of a single client, or whether it spans the market and therefore offers a wider potential customer base. Further networking (including internal) can unearth where other clients in other industries may have similar, albeit not identical, issues. Their resilience and belief in their idea should enable them to come at the solution from multiple angles, to be able to have multiple and repeated conversations with clients before they get a sale, and to retain the momentum for the project. They need to just be able to keep going.

We have an interested client, now what? Minimum Viable Products and managing expectations

This is another part of the education piece. Again, another sweeping generalization that lawyers tend not to approach their clients with anything other than a complete and perfect solution – which is always a problem as it assumes that perfect is entirely achievable. As part of the education process, it is key to work out whose definition you are using for complete and perfect. The answer, of course, should be the end user, meaning the client and not necessarily the subject matter expert. This is why it is so essential to involve the client in the process and start with the creation of an MVP rather than wait until the end product. Once you have enough to show to a client (i.e., an MVP), then you can start conversations as to whether they think the solution will work and what changes they might like to make, which in turn leads to conversations about how long those changes might take and any compromises between a perfect version compared to one that will actually achieve the client's outcome. Something both the client and your lawyers need to accept is that there is no completely perfect for any given value of perfect.

Let us be honest here – and we say this as former practicing lawyers – there is no perfect legal advice, no perfect contract, no perfect lease, no perfect settlement – but different standards seem to apply as soon as you stray outside of what may be regarded as "traditional legal advice". We have had to run (time consuming) A/B tests to prove to our skeptics that some of our technology solutions perform as well as or (more usually) better than a human-driven solution.

Indeed, our starting point when it comes to technology-led innovation is that human beings do not produce perfect results (the first ten years of one of our careers as a professional indemnity lawyer was spent representing lawyers who had produced allegedly imperfect, and, indeed some actually imperfect results). We refer to Moravec's paradox, which is named after Hans Moravec, a robotics expert and artificial intelligence researcher who first proposed the idea in the 1980s. Moravec's Paradox states that the things that are easy for humans, such as perception, creativity, and social interaction, are hard for computers, while the things that are difficult for humans, such as mathematical calculations and logical reasoning, are easy for computers. This paradox arises because the human brain has evolved to perform tasks that were essential for our survival as a species, such as navigating complex environments, interacting with other humans, and recognizing patterns in the natural world. These are tasks that are (or at least historically were) difficult to program into a computer, while mathematical and logical tasks can be easily automated.

So, while humans have a comparative advantage in tasks that require common sense, intuition, and social skills, computers have a comparative advantage in tasks that require processing vast amounts of data and performing complex calculations. Thus, in tasks that require lawyers to undertake repeatable and predictable activities over long period of time, such as document review, it should not be a surprise that document review systems can outperform humans. Humans get tired, distracted, and categorize things differently between themselves and in some cases are not consistent from an individual either. So our starting point is not that the technology has to be perfect, it just has to be at least equal to that which has gone before. In tasks such as document review, it really should not be a surprise that technology outperforms humans in terms of accuracy, speed, and consistency over long periods of time. Yes, it will miss things, yes, it will get things wrong, but so do people – the question is whether the solution is better or worse.

In the urgent document review case study detailed above, we undertook this over a two-week period. Because of the volume of documents involved, the client instructed us to review half of the documents and another firm the other half. We used a combination of technology and humans to provide the output. In our own, internal, A/B test, we found that this combination (compared to using humans alone) reduced the time involved in reviewing documents by 90 percent (savings we passed on to the client). In addition, the client audited the output of both firms and reported that our output had an accuracy of 98 percent. The firm that approached the exercise without technology scored much lower, and we were able to take on some of the document reviews that they could not complete. This, and similar, examples evidence our hypothesis that applying technology to repeatable and predictable tasks improves the accuracy of the output and reduces the time taken to get it. Showcasing case studies like this can help in managing expectations and overcoming skepticism.

Is it repeatable and scalable (and does it always matter)?

We have found this something of a challenge. It is one thing to get something up and running as an MVP for a particular client and bask in the reflected glory of a job well done, but the real aim of this sort of innovation is to turn that idea into a product you can sell on to other clients with similar problems and benefit further from the initial investment. This is a difficult step to achieve. For example, for our HR app mentioned above we set up nearly 10,000 user accounts, which we had to do the hard way by adding users in batches of 100 with an agreed set of introductory text – which is hardly scalable. Similarly, we configured the app to work with the specific client's internal process, which is not easily repeatable and scalable for each client. We made a version of the tool without any client-specific references to show to other clients, which is now getting traction. We worked out several levels of pricing for our solutions, including pricing for client-specific changes or white labelling, all with the view of reflecting some of the additional work such changes entail.

At the risk of stating the obvious, the decision to make something repeatable and scalable does come down to some basics. What revenue do you think can be generated from the solution? What net profit target do you need to meet, and can you afford to resource the solution and still deliver the net profit? If you cannot, by definition, your solution is not scalable so you will need to accept this or think of another way of doing it.

It does not always matter if something is repeatable and scalable. All law firms will have a number of clients for which it is simply worthwhile as part of the ongoing relationship to develop solutions for those clients regardless. However, the firm must accept that this approach cannot apply to all clients. This comes back in part to prioritization. Whilst all clients are equal, some are more equal than others in this context.

Chapter checklist

- ☐ Can you identify any common characteristics in projects that have been successful in your organization?
- ☐ Can you identify strong subject matter experts, who display not just technical excellence but a broader spread of skills that is likely to assist your innovation efforts? How can you upskill those who show potential?
- ☐ Do you routinely get the right mix of people working on projects in your organization? If not, what can you do to change this?
- ☐ Have you got or can you create a process for getting to a minimal viable product (MVP)?

References

1 A "reserve" on a claim is the amount that the insurer needs to set aside to cover settlement of that claim and, when instructed, one of the roles of acting for insurers in these sorts of claims is for the lawyer to advise the insurer on the size of the reserve the insurer needs to set aside to cover the claim. Reserves on all of the claims that the insurer knows about are aggregated so that the insurer has enough money to meet its financial obligations to its policyholders.

2 See: www.weightmans.com/products/predict/

3 A former managing partner of a law firm once described their role as "largely making sure there was an equality of low-level unhappiness across the business".

Chapter 6:

Change management – dealing with people

So, you have decided to start on some innovation projects and you are excited to get going. This excitement is slowly tempered by the dawning realization that bringing others along with change of any description is a hard slog. There are many weighty texts on the theory and practice of change management, which we are not proposing to regurgitate (some are definitely worth a read, others less so) but the sheer volume of them, together with the numbers of consultants who purport to be able to help organizations manage change, should act as a warning sign that this is not going to be a walk in the park. In many respects, the technology and process aspects of innovation are the easy part. This chapter is all about people, and we all know there are many strong-willed people in law firms! This is often set against a background that those who are interested in innovation may not readily identify as "people people" (certainly us!) so requires extra effort and planning. This chapter outlines some of the characters you are likely to come across whilst delivering innovation projects and some suggestions on how to most effectively engage (or not, let's pick our battles!) with them.

Of course, as people we are multi-faceted and there is every chance that a person displays multiple characteristics (or that even on different projects people display different characteristics). This is all part of the glorious world of change, and you need to roll with it. Repeat after me: "This is not personal" (even though it may feel like it). As with most things people related, a lot of this is how you choose to react, accepting that you cannot choose how others show up. In Figure 1, we've grouped the personas from hardest to easiest to deal with (of course, this may be different for you!) and we've tended to find that many of the characteristics overlap so if one suggestion is not working, try pivoting and using the suggestions from others in the same column.

Hardest

- The "I've promised the client an app for that" lawyer
- The naysayer
- The keyboard warrior
- The obdurate litigator
- The "That should be free for my client" lawyer

Medium

- The enthusiastic amateur
- The "Can we have an app for that" lawyer
- The technology visionary
- The overcommitted lawyer

Easiest

- The baffled-by-Excel lawyer
- The only interested the week before their appraisal lawyer
- The gold dust lawyer

Figure 1. The relative ease of dealing with colleagues

The "I've promised the client an app for that" lawyer

Characteristics

Sometimes related to the *"Can we have an app for that"* persona (see below), this is the kind of person who tells you that an app has been promised to a client, and you then have to work out: (i) what, if anything, has been said and promised to the client; and (ii) is an app even the best solution? As a sweeping generalization, this character is usually quite senior and experienced in dealing with clients; often unaccustomed to being told "no" and does not want to disappoint the client. These added complications mean navigating this persona can be difficult. It is also generally the case that they have made the offer in a panicked moment when they have been asked what they can do to help the client around technology and innovation.

Frequent phrases

- *"I spoke with [client] and we agree that an app would solve this. I said they can have it by [insert ridiculously short timeline], for free (and please carry on with delivery of my other urgent matters)."*

How to navigate them

This is a tricky one to navigate. The intention of the lawyer when they offered an app as a solution can be equally tricky to ascertain. You will want to quickly get to the bottom of the position with the client. This requires you to take a step back and work out: (i) what has gone on; (ii) what has been promised; and (iii) the impact on other projects. Enlist others to help – those that know the client or have been in the meetings, and those in an innovation team who would be tasked with delivery. Crawl through any meeting notes or documents (of course, there is the very slim prospect that all of this will have been clearly documented in apple pie order, ready for a business service team to deliver it – we've never been lucky enough to have that scenario) and then form a small group to review them and understand what the client needs and what was offered. Much will depend upon whether they have been having the conversation with the right people at the client end – have two lawyers essentially got excited and come up with ideas that may not be feasible, or have they started to involve process or technology people?

What happens next depends upon, first, whether the idea is in any way feasible. Assuming it is, you then need to see if you have resources to deliver the project. If you can, or if scoping it out further is advantageous, then you are often looking to get back to the original discussion of the problem and a chance to workshop with the client. A lot of this depends upon how it is positioned (both internally and externally). With clients, it can often be positioned positively as an opportunity to have a detail-based, user-centric workshop involving the technical experts from the client and law firm, where you can explore the problem from their perspective without approaching it with a fixed solution. Often, this brings different problems to the surface that you can help solve, rather than the one you have been presented with where the solution is to "app" it!. You can then work to break the delivery down into achievable milestone chunks.

How you deal with this internally depends mainly on whether the person is a repeat offender or not:

- *This is not a repeat offender.* Occasionally, this situation results from a genuine keenness to deliver for clients, coupled with a lack of awareness of internal processes, particularly that the firm's business services organization is not a free, unlimited, and underutilized resource. This gives you the opportunity to revisit your internal messaging to see if it could be communicated differently:

- Do people know how to contact your team and who to contact? Do your people respond in a timely manner or does stuff fall into a black hole?
- Do you share the headlines of your processes so people can understand how things are done?
- How do you raise awareness and communicate with the wider firm? Do you put information and updates in firm-wide communications? Do you attend team or practice group meetings or do roadshows in different offices? We accept all of this takes time and resource, both of which are often in short supply in innovation teams, but periodically it is important to step back and review processes, including communications, especially as teams grow and mature. We have tended to use the addition of a new team member(s) as an opportunity to review (before they start) existing roles and responsibilities.[1]

- *This is a repeat offender.* No matter how clear your messaging on processes, or how available you make yourself, there is always a cohort who will not operate that way. They promise things to clients as a way of frustrating the prioritization processes and use early client involvement to do this. Queue jumping is a perennial problem in product and innovation in a law firm. Naturally, everyone thinks their client is the most important and no one wants to let their clients down, but you need to think of what message this behavior sends in your organization if the request is acceded to. There must be some form of consequence to ensure they do not repeat the offence or, worse, encourage others to do it so that delivery suddenly becomes uncontrollable. This often requires senior people helping you to reconfirm messaging.

Of course, innovation by its very nature is dynamic, but you want to ensure you are involved at the right stage so you can facilitate understanding the problem and solutions before the unfeasible is promised, so that the delivery can be balanced and prioritized against everything else.

The naysayer

Characteristics

The naysayer gives something only one chance in a technology context. No matter how new it is or how unique their use case, it must be perfect. If it does not work to their level of satisfaction (or they cannot get it to work) that is it, forever. They are usually vocal about other things in an organization and sure of their beliefs.

Frequent phrases

- *"This did not work once so it will never work, for anyone, ever, and I am going to tell this to everyone I meet."*
- *"The [insert name of document automation system] does not do me a perfect first draft every time because in circumstances that I cannot explain, I need a different clause and it does not do it."* (Note – this is usually a one-in-a-million event and requires the stars and everything else to align.)
- *"I saw similar technology in 2018 and it was not perfect then – if it is not perfect now why would I want to look at it?"*
- *"Fundamentally I do not understand how you think that technology can be better than or even help me with what I do on a day-to-day basis."*
- *"How can technology be better at tasks than my lawyers?" (seemingly oblivious to the fact that his/her team of lawyers who, after all, are human, might make mistakes).*

How to navigate them

We all know that not every pilot will be a success, nor will every piece of technology work in the way you want or expect. In this scenario, negative comment is to be expected; lessons are to be learned and shared and you try something else, or explain the developments since they last saw it. Sometimes a successful pilot on a different use case is enough to spur people to try again.

The naysayer is different because they are usually expecting unparalleled levels of success from a piece of technology, which is usually out of kilter with the expectations of the human equivalent. Imagine giving a contract to a more junior colleague to draft. Unless you have given them a precedent and a specific set of instructions, you are not likely to get a contract that is exactly how you would draft it. You might make some amends to the document but are probably not going to rewrite every word and you will live with the contract having a comma where you wouldn't have put one or a sentence not quite how you would have written it (or not, depending on predilection). The naysayer expects the technology to replicate what they would do as if they are the only technology user. In the document automation context as an example, unless the technology gives them a version using the style and syntax they would have used, then it is deemed a failure. You've got to compare apples with apples and pears with pears. If the thing in question isn't tailored to the individual idiosyncrasy of the individual lawyer it is deemed by them to be a failure, even when from a legal perspective the output is perfectly "good".

How you deal with them depends whether they are a senior, vocal but likely to be a non-user of the technology, or someone who is more likely to be using the technology day-to-day:

- *Likely non-user:* You do not need to turn everyone into technology and innovation evangelists, but they do need to give new concepts a chance, especially if they are not the ultimate end user of the technology. For example, a partner may not use a piece of document automation software, but it may be of great assistance for a more junior colleague to get them a working first draft. It is then unhelpful if said partner changes every word of the draft or talks openly about how poor quality the first draft is (made even more annoying if they had been part of a group of lawyers tasked with agreeing precedents to then automate). The old adage of "If you haven't got anything nice[2] to say, please don't say anything" is one worth repeating. You may need some senior buy-in to help with this messaging to encourage only constructive comments.
- *Likely user:* You have to try and get to the bottom of the disquiet. If you have involved them in the planning and pilots, then the opportunity for this to arise should be minimized. It may transpire that the technology is the final straw and not the underlying problem. Again, you may need some senior buy-in to help with the messaging.

The keyboard warrior

Characteristics

We all know someone that causes us to let out a little sigh as their email arrives in our inboxes. In the world of innovation, there is often more than one, so prepare yourself. You know the email will be an overly long way to make any point, and often hostile and combative in approach. When you read it, you must remind yourself that you both work at the same firm and want the project to be a success. Remember the mantra, "It isn't personal".

Their email warrior skills have often been honed over years of attritional exchanges with the other side and they carry this on with internal emails as it has become entrenched behavior. Ironically, they often lack the technical knowledge of the business services aspect of a project, but this does not stop them launching into a verbose response where every email you send is seen as a threat and an opportunity for them to demonstrate their advocacy skills. They have deep legal knowledge but shallow experience in anything else and assume they can make up for that lack of experience through sheer force of intellect and their version of what they regard as "common sense". Not a persona with an abundance of self-awareness as a rule.

Frequent phrases

- *"What does [insert name of managing partner] say?" (usually whilst copying another 50 partners into an email chain).*
- *"I am not trying to be difficult but..."*
- *"(I do not understand this but) I fail to see how this is so hard."*

How to navigate them

Ring them (yes, old-fashioned phone!). I appreciate that in the early days this is easier said than done and will require all your steely resolve as you don't know if the call will disarm or enflame until you've made it. As a rule (albeit not 100 percent foolproof), even the most vitriolic and supercilious of keyboard warriors tend not to be able to keep that attitude up in the face of a real, live human being. That is partly why they resorted to email in the first place. Even someone who starts off as hostile on a call can usually be persuaded after a couple of minutes of animated discussion. Ringing them (especially if not booked as a meeting so they can plan) takes the wind out of their sails and disarms them. It is much easier to tell them verbally that they have the wrong end of the stick than to email it (as there are usually many others copied into the thread by now) and you often earn their respect as they realize you have saved them embarrassment in the email thread.

Ever-increasing email chains are unlikely to help in the long run and need the sting taking out of them. Use the rule of four: if you are about to send the fourth email in the chain, you clearly are not getting through and it needs a discussion. You are collectively failing to communicate using the written word (frequently because the correspondents are working with a different set of assumptions, so you may not even be arguing about the same thing). One method is to simply say it will be easier to discuss and set up a meeting. You then need to think about who to have in the meeting. Is this character like this with everyone? Is there a colleague who may be better at explaining things to them? Does level of seniority matter? Don't take it personally. Easier said than done. You might also want to think about calling the person to whom they report, just to warn them that this appears to be an issue and ask if they are comfortable with you dealing with it. It pays for them to have heard your side before they hear from someone who is worked up. As a form of communication, email is open to far too much interpretation, both in terms of the actual content and, more importantly, the intent behind it.

The obdurate litigator

Characteristics

This persona is common in law firms and should be expected. After all, lawyers are trained to argue, and to argue well throughout their career, keen to win for their clients. This person is vocal and verbose in written and oral advocacy. This person regards email as a combat sport and even when they write what they consider measured and reasonable emails, they can nevertheless be received as hostile. They are much more comfortable with confrontation than most and pepper emails with many unnecessary capital letters.

Frequent phrases

- *"Why not do it how I suggested?"*
- *"I know you have done the research, but they are my clients and I know what they want."*
- *Starts and ends formally "Dear xxx, yours sincerely YYY."*

How to navigate them

This is a difficult character if you encounter them early on, as all you are trying to do is help and it often feels that you are dealing with an opponent rather than someone in the same firm. It is especially difficult because you are still trying to work it all out, so someone strongly suggesting another way is not always helpful. These people are very vocal in meetings when detailing their suggestion and will not countenance any other view, also meaning if you start to ask questions about their suggestion, these are rapidly shut down. Their position may soften as you go through a project and can demonstrate progress (but don't bank on it!).

In this situation, thorough preparation is your friend. Prep widely – about the idea, the external market, and the client. If you frame this character in a positive light, then all their opposition can be used to help you hone your problem-solving and negotiation skills. As you already know you are going to face challenge, as part of your preparation you can plan many different scenarios so you can anticipate the push back and how to deal with it. In the same way that the obdurate litigator wants to be right, you have to make sure you do not fall into the same trap. Innovation relies a lot on the art of humble enquiry and empathetic listening, and you need to be able to give them a graceful way to change their mind without it feeling like you are undermining their original, authoritatively stated position. You need to be the adult in the room. Here is your opportunity to practice this.

Getting others on side (particularly those to whom they report) is also a useful way of maneuvering this person to a different viewpoint, but it can be slow. This may involve pre-meeting meetings to present your plan to get others on board with it before the main discussion.

The "That should be free for my client" lawyer

Characteristics

Regardless of whether this character is keen on innovation or not, they want to ensure the innovation or product in question is free for their client, regardless of how vocal they have been previously in making sure there was a clear ROI for innovation that must be measured in monetary terms. The problem with this type of behavior is that it rapidly catches on and suddenly there are a number of similar requests.

Frequent phrases

- *"I know we usually charge for this but my client is [so important/about to send us more work/we need to cement relationships/about to run a tender process etc.] that I told them I am not going to charge them."*
- *"We have already built it so there is no cost involved in giving it to my client, surely?"*
- *"Given the amount of work we get from this client, we cannot possibly charge them for this."*

How to navigate them

It is really disheartening to see innovation considered as a "value add" rather than as a way of delivering modern legal services, particularly when the proponent in question would think nothing of charging every minute of lawyer time on a matter. "Value add" is of course an oxymoron; the very definition of "value" is something that the client would pay for, but we digress. Of course, there will be many occasions where the innovation or product may not be directly charged, but there is indirect revenue that can nonetheless be tracked – for example, winning a pitch due to the innovation demonstrated – and it is important to capture these as part of reporting back internally so that your organization can see the value of the innovation team.

Navigating this kind of behavior usually requires senior buy-in to set some rules around what is value add and what is not and, crucially, who makes those decisions and how. It can sometimes be helpful to explain that there is an underlying cost that the business should be recouping from: (i) the upfront effort to build the solution; (ii) the ongoing effort to support the solution; and (iii) the future efforts to improve the solution over time. It can be helpful to put a monetary cost on this and relate it back to the cost of a lawyer's time in which you are not paying for the time per se as much as using that as a way of valuing the years of experience that the lawyer brings to their clients. If they sell the solution, it can help if that sale counts in some way towards their revenue targets and the profitability targets for the work done for that client.

The enthusiastic amateur

Characteristics

There are usually a couple of enthusiastic amateurs around; they are often quite interested in technology in general and in terms of law technology and innovation may have done some wider reading or taken themselves off to an event. They possibly read and watch science fiction movies and always have the latest gadget.

Frequent phrases

- *"When I went to [insert conference name] I met..."*
- *"I love wandering round on the metaverse."*
- *"Have you seen this...?"*
- *"I saw a demo of X and thought it was great. I have asked them to speak to you so we can get some licenses."*

How to navigate them

Innovation is a people game and you are always going to be short of messengers, so being able to harness keen people can be useful. What is important is that their keenness is tempered to help facilitate what you are actually trying to achieve. By all means they can share their ideas with the innovation team, but you do not want everyone thinking that their latest interest is going to solve every problem. In a similar vein, they are often quite keen on signing up to demos or getting demos arranged following conferences – the trick is to pair them up with someone in the innovation team who can sit through the demos too and then talk them through the steps needed to pilot technology in a law firm.

The "Can we have an app for that" lawyer

Characteristics

There are some people that, once they have an idea in their head, it becomes the answer to everything, as is often the case with this persona. Regardless of whether they have been fast or slow to adopt innovation, they believe that there is only one way of solving any problem, and that is to create an app (or five)!

Frequent phrases

- *"I think this could be an app" – often as an answer to any potential problem.*
- *"Our competitors have got apps, what apps do we have for our clients?"*
- *"What we need is a place where we can put all of these apps together. Maybe we could build an app store?"*

How to navigate them

Hearing, "I think this could be an app" is sometimes a blessing or a curse. It is, of course, great that people are thinking about where technology could be used to enhance legal services and some of the suggestions are good. However, some are not so good and you need to get to a point quickly where you can filter out the helpful from the unhelpful. Factors to explore include:

- *Is the issue in question both scalable and repeatable?* For "scalable", this means it would apply to more than one client, project, or piece of work to justify the resource (there may be occasional cases where scalability does not matter as the size of the initial prize makes it worth doing, but these instances are few and far between – think two or fewer a year depending on the size of your team and/or firm). For repeatable, this means there needs to be a way of working out the answer that is capable of replication – that is, 50 lawyers might all go about it a different way and come to different conclusions, all of which could be equally right.

- *The legal framework.* Is it capable of a yes/no/maybe answer where there are key factors that are capable of being defined in such a way as to result in an answer to a question? There are also occasions where finding the "grey" decisions are helpful. This is often the case where the decision in the middle requires someone with more experience or expertise to deal with them. In these circumstances, an app can be useful to filter out the extreme ends (for example, strong grounds to defend or admit), which means that the more obvious (less grey) cases can be dealt with by different colleagues and the grey ones by colleagues with more experience or more specialist experience. Fraud flags (i.e. potential factors that may be indicative of fraud that means further, specialist, investigation is warranted) in litigated claims could be an example of this.
- *Who usually does this type of legal work?* If it is paralegals or junior lawyers, you are more likely to be able to incorporate or convert it into an app as there should be a framework that is explained to those doing the work. You would hope.
- *Is anyone really going to download and use it?* Look at your own smartphone. How many of your downloaded apps do you actually use beyond your essentials? Can you remember what all of the apps do? Is the use case for this app one that means that clients will actually use it? An app from a law firm? Really? (Yawn).

The fact that this person thinks of apps as the solution to everything is, in itself, a positive start and much like the technology visionary, there are some steps you can take to push them into thinking a bit broader. Starting with a client or user focus and asking, "What is the problem you are trying to solve?" (sound familiar?) can be helpful. Sometimes, explaining different types of technology and some examples of how it has been used is enough to get them thinking a little differently. Much like the person who has a hammer and thinks everything looks like a nail, you need to push this person out of their comfort zone to think a bit differently.

The technology visionary

Characteristics

This person is excited by technology but cannot actually explain how it will help. They often pick up all of the buzzwords and scatter them liberally throughout any prose or conversation. They also spotted the last big thing and did nothing with that either. However, this is a great person to have on side from the beginning. They love a buzzword and are good at remembering them – the issue is usually the context and the other words they put around them. Whilst not naturally the most technology-capable, they are a powerful ally because they see the longer-term vision too. They often have a lot of business experience and the foresight to see how the world, especially for clients, will look in the future. What they can struggle with is articulating that overall vision into a roadmap with various stages that actually enables operational teams to understand, let alone deliver, them. This means they can start more projects than is ever likely to be possible and can appear quite fickle, so competing resources for different projects becomes a problem.

There is a sense of urgency with a technology visionary which, at the organizational level, is helpful to encourage action and galvanize discussions. However, they view anything related to technology or innovation as urgent and often struggle to prioritize projects to work on and areas to explore.

As a generalization, they are usually also people people with wide internal and external networks – both a blessing and a curse as you find yourself in meetings with people spouting random buzzwords. With some upskilling and support they can be a powerful ally – you certainly do not want to dampen their enthusiasm (starting off, we need all the supporters we can muster).

Frequent phrases

- *"Can we blockchain this?"*
- *"Legal services of the future will look like [buzzword 1] with a strong emphasis on [buzzword 2].[3] We should make it happen!"*
- *"What are we doing about [insert the latest media hype]? All our competitors and clients are all over this."*
- *"Susskind predicts technology will be our demise, what is our strategy for dealing with that?"*
- *"We need an end-to-end, always-on, self-service solution for our clients."*

How to navigate them

This is a tricky one as in the hearts and minds battle you are going to need all the help you can get, and you do not want to discourage potential supporters or champions, so handle this person with care. However, you also do not want to go into every meeting wondering what version of buzzword bingo you will be playing or spending a lot of time on corrections.

Upskilling is a useful way of harnessing the positive aspects of this characteristic, but has to be done in the right way. There is no point providing an in-depth technical explanation. You need readily accessible reference sheets that use the language of features, benefits, and value – the more you can make this client focused and with examples, the better. You want to be the one providing the buzzwords, but in the correct context. Grouping ideas or types of technology into "buckets" or presenting it in a menu-style format can also be helpful ways of supporting this person to usefully champion things.

This person usually has very in-depth client knowledge so spending time with them will pay dividends. Whilst they cannot always express the solution in the correct terminology, they are usually very adept at enunciating the client problem or telling you how their clients' market is evolving. Understanding this not only helps you deal with the area in which the person is the expert, but can also give you ideas of how to explore such conversations with people who are less adept at this and can join up ideas. For example, it is unlikely that there is only one sector of clients who have issues with contract lifecycle management, so an understanding from one client can help with discussions with others. In the early days, you need to try and ensure that this person is not so far ahead in their visionary thinking that it becomes unrelatable for those they work with and means they cannot bring colleagues on the journey with them. If all else fails, amuse yourself and play meeting buzzword bingo.

The overcommitted lawyer

Characteristics

There have been several studies written about the personalities of lawyers.[4] Usually, they find that lawyers have a similar personality type of an insecure overachiever, which manifests itself as continual worry that they have not quite worked hard enough for their clients. This, in our experience (and as a sweeping generalization), means that they are very poor at saying "no" to clients and to work. Coupled with an ambitious drive for the next promotion, it is not hard to see how lawyers end up overcommitted in terms of work, clients, team, or management responsibilities.

Frequent phrases

- *"Is this ok next month?"*
- *"It is on my list, I will certainly get to it by X [insert ridiculously unachievable timescale]."*

How to navigate them

Typically, the overcommitted lawyer falls into one of two camps:

1. Genuinely busy but does get to everything (eventually) and wants to be involved.
2. Genuinely busy but rarely does what they say and, even if they want to be involved, are unlikely to ever offer anything practical other than platitudes.

Clearly, one of these groupings will work out for you (even if eventually) and the other will not. It is important to quickly ascertain which type you are dealing with so that you can pick the right tactic. For those in the second category, offer platitudes back but do not factor them into your project planning to avoid disappointment. Trust your instincts here; speak to others and look at past behavior as a predictor. You are not going to change them.

You stand more chance of some useful involvement with the first group, but you need to plan carefully.

- *Great expectations:* This person's expectations are likely to be great in terms of the time involvement needed or their impact on the overall project. They imagine the thing requires more of their time than it does so they put it off until some mythical future period when this time will suddenly become available to them, despite all prior experience to the contrary. Sometimes, overcommitted lawyers are not the best at accurately working out the amount of time or effort required to do something. Anything that you can do to clarify, such as providing time estimates, is likely to be gratefully received and may even see your project moved up the list. It is good to show your work is not something that needs to go on the enormous pile.
- *Pillar and post:* You have often got into your current innovation roles by knowing a lot of people in the firm and how the firm works. What is taking up the overcommitted lawyer's time? Is there a quid pro quo

– can you help them to do something in a better way, for example? Are they spending time reviewing data or compiling a spreadsheet that could be partially automated?

- *Crucial or nice to have?* Many of us suffer from meeting fatigue. Can you be more judicious with meeting arrangements and time spent in them compared to the outcomes? Do we just invite certain people to meetings because of habit? With the "overcommitted but gets there in the end" lawyer, you want their input where it has the most impact – such as reviewing a document after several drafts rather than being involved with the drafting.
- *Pay it forward:* The overcommitted lawyer is in demand because they are good. Have they got a capable junior colleague who can attend meetings for them and then involve the overcommitted lawyer at the right moment? This also has the advantage of spreading the innovation message and upskilling more of the firm for future projects: win-win!

The baffled-by-Excel lawyer

Characteristics

Historically, being a lawyer was about knowing the law, or where to find it, and business and people skills were less of a given. The advent of the "T shaped",[5] "O shaped",[6] and "LawPlus"[7] models shows us that these days being a lawyer is about so much more than finding, understanding, and applying the law. Regardless of whether they are a new entrant or a seasoned professional, if the person thinks very rigidly of the job as only being about law, then tools like Excel are a mystery to them, let alone AI. This person often displays a fixed mindset and rigid thinking, making them reluctant to consider the advantages of innovation. On a change curve they would be permanently stuck in denial.[8] Incredulity drips from this character, especially in relation to the speed of adoption of technology and new ways of working by their organization. But, almost paradoxically, they are someone who struggles with change in general and never attends any innovation sessions or training, especially if they are part of a pilot.

Frequent phrases

- *"My client would not be interested in that, they are like me and like reading my long client reports."*

- *"I did not go to law school to have to use Excel, that is someone else's job."*
- *"My area of law is particularly esoteric and not susceptible to assistance from technology and innovation. I understand it works for all other practice areas in the firm, but it cannot possibly be relevant to my area."*
- *"We have done it successfully like this for the last 20 years, and my clients are perfectly happy with the way in which I am doing it; or at least they have not told me they are not happy."*
- *'We put a person on the moon over 50 years ago, how can we possibly not be able to do X, Y, or Z?'*

How to navigate them

Whilst everyone has the capacity to change, there is certainly a group of people who will try to avoid it. Some, dare we say, are hoping to eke out the last few years of their career without having to embrace anything new. You need to weigh up the time and effort involved in forcing change upon them against a likely minimal gain in terms of attitude or engagement. This is likely to feel immensely frustrating and that you are fighting a losing battle. If they have a client you want to work with or a particular area of work in which you are exploring innovation, then you will make your life easier by involving their colleagues who are more change minded. Work with people who want to work with you – you only have a finite resource after all.

The only interested the week before their appraisal lawyer

Characteristics

This one has always amused us. The first time it happened, we did not see it for what it was. We got seemingly random requests from a number of people all within a couple of weeks of each other, having never heard from them before. They wanted to "have a chat", which invariably ended with them telling us how they thought they could do innovation better. We did not make the same mistake the next year and the team were warned to anticipate a sudden, fleeting, surge of interest. Of course, no one minds helping people increase their prospect of being promoted – but it is better to be prepared for what to expect.

Frequent phrases

- *"Can I grab an hour and get up to speed on ALL of your innovation projects?"*
- *"[In interview] I've spoken to innovation about my idea [aka I asked them an unrelated question once in passing] and they said it is brilliant!"*
- *"I've been working with the innovation team on X."*[9]

How to navigate them

This can be a tricky persona to handle, especially in your early days. You need to quickly ascertain whether they are purely trying to extract some information from you to drop into their application or interview, or whether they have a genuine idea. If the former, schedule a time-limited chat, or have an email prepared, where you direct them to stock materials. If you have an innovation team, then you all need to be saying the same message – you do not want them taking up hours of your colleagues' time either if they find it harder to say "no".

If they come with a vaguely coherent idea then you need to ascertain if this is worth exploring, and to what level. As a general predictor of future involvement, asking for a discussion early in the process is more likely to bear fruit than a phone call the week before a deadline. Honesty usually works best too, so do not be afraid to ask if it is an idea they have a long-term commitment to, or if it is a fleeting interview fancy and await the nervous laughter. If there is a genuine keenness, treat it as you would any other project.[10]

The gold dust lawyer

Characteristics

As mythical as a unicorn, the gold dust lawyer is, as the name suggests, exceptionally rare. They are the perfect mix of legal knowledge, client contact, and creative problem solving. They are good at joining up the dots (and silos) in organizations. They are networked internally and externally as they are good with people and pleasant to work with. They know what they know and what they do not know and are keen to learn more. They understand that there are, whisper it, professionals in law firms who: (i) are not lawyers; (ii) do not want to be a lawyer; (iii) have experience in domains that the lawyers do not have; and (iv) can offer value to lawyers from other specialisms, be that HR, marketing, IT or, indeed, innovation.

Frequent phrases

- *"I have been thinking about X idea and sounded a client out. Can I work with the team to see if it is feasible? How can I help?"*
- *"Who else will be useful to get involved in this?"*
- *"Where else in the firm might this work?"*
- *"I know someone who might help with this."*

How to navigate them

When you find this character, do everything in your power to support and champion them! You will wish you could clone them and, whilst this isn't possible, you can try to mix them with others who show evidence of some of the same potential in the hope that they can learn from them. They are usually keen to run with every project they possibly can and step in to save things – it is important to try and ensure they are not involved in everything and have some time to think and join the innovation dots.

Chapter checklist

- ☐ How would you rate your stakeholder management skills and those of your team?
- ☐ Do you recognize any of the caricatures in your organization?
- ☐ Can you map your stakeholders against the ease of dealing with them?
- ☐ Do your stakeholders demonstrate different traits in different projects?
- ☐ Who in your organization can help you navigate stakeholders?

References

1 We do a "start/stop/continue" of how a job description has morphed into what people actually do. Are the team doing stuff they find interesting, have they been promoted and outgrown some things, do they need a different challenge? When the new team member starts, we try and find out what processes have worked for them previously in other organisations in which they have worked, how do they work, how their skills fit into the wider team, how they can help with refining ways of working (especially if they bring fresh eyes from not working in a law firm). Process refinement is iterative so using online collaboration tools allow you to modify them without too much hassle.

2 Or at the very least, constructive.

3 Which has no natural link to [buzzword 1].

4 MacEwen, B., "Growth is Dead: Part 7- Psychology" 21 October 2012. See: https://adamsmithesq.com/2012/10/growth-is-dead-part-7/.

5 Mak, E., "The T-shaped Lawyer and Beyond: Rethinking legal professionalism and legal education for contemporary societies", June 2017. See: www.researchgate.net/profile/Elaine-Mak/publication/331022253_The_T-shaped_Lawyer_and_Beyond_Rethinking_legal_professionalism_and_legal_education_for_contemporary_societies/links/5c619ca5a6fdccb608bb961f/The-T-shaped-Lawyer-and-Beyond-Rethinking-legal-professionalism-and-legal-education-for-contemporary-societies.pdf

6 See: https://oshaped.com/the-o-shaped-mindset-and-attributes

7 Curphey, A., *The Legal Team of the Future: Law+ Skills*, London: London Publishing Partnership, 2022.

8 The change curve was original developed by Elisabeth Kubler-Ross to explain the grieving process. It is also used to help explain reactions to change. See: www.ekrfoundation.org/5-stages-of-grief/change-curve/.

9 Translation: "I had one tentative conversation with the innovation team and will drop all interest as quickly as is humanly possible if I am promoted."

10 PS, if you are this person, we do check whether what you are saying has any substance to it as part of the interview process.

Chapter 7:
So, you want me to collaborate?

Technology is often the easiest part of solving a problem. If you have started reading this book from the beginning, you will have noticed that we have spent a lot of pages talking about people; whether that be building a team or the attitudes towards innovation that you are likely to encounter along the way. Collaboration is another facet of the people side of innovation and takes many forms. We have always found that innovation works best when we collaborate with clients, technology suppliers, academics, and our people, and when we underpin that collaboration with a process, of which technology plays a part. Whilst collaboration is often crucial for successful innovation, it can take some careful managing. This chapter explores some of the highs and lows of different collaboration scenarios.

Internal collaboration – working with lawyers and business services

In theory, this should be easy, after all, you are all at the same firm, with the same purpose and clients. However, in practice, whilst you all share the same overall goal, everyone has a different understanding and idea of how best to achieve that goal – informed by their own experiences and specialism on an individual, department, or group level. Lawyers can be quite protective of their clients, to the extent they may be reluctant to facilitate access to other lawyer colleagues, let alone those in business services (the aforementioned "nons" i.e. "non-lawyers" who cannot possibly be expected to know how to talk to clients and what to say and not to say). There is definitely a ripple effect if you can break down the barriers though and this then becomes a good group to sound out ideas or to hear what the market is doing.

Collaborating with lawyers – what works?

Through a process of trial and error, we have identified some of the key factors that are more likely than not to make collaboration with your subject matter expert lawyers that little bit easier. You are unlikely to get all the attributes that would be helpful in one individual,[1] and there is usually likely to be a trade-off. For the sake of your innovation team, you want to try and ensure it is not always the same attribute missing for all the subject matter experts, or this can mean a lot of difficult projects on the go at the same time. As we detailed in earlier chapters, innovation is uncomfortable enough when it is your full-time job, let alone when you are a lawyer dipping into projects. It is incumbent that, as an innovation team, you hold people's hands through the process and never underestimate the level of challenge in what you are asking people to do. Just because it becomes second nature to you doing it day in and day out does not mean it is similarly so for a lawyer on a project. Patience and empathy are required – if you find yourself running low on either, then it is time to swap with a colleague with a little more bounce at that particular moment. Here are some tips we have picked up along the way to smooth the path of collaboration.

The right lawyer

It is a trite observation that not all lawyers are created equal, and you only need to look through some of the headings in chapter six to appreciate that you may encounter challenging people who are unaccustomed to not being the decision maker. This makes selecting "the right lawyer" to collaborate with very important. This is especially the case if an innovation function and the related roles are new in your organization – you do not want the innovation team to be disengaged before you have even started due to negative interactions with lawyers. So what characteristics does "the right lawyer" have?

- *Subject matter expert*. This does not mean the lawyer has to be a partner. The domain knowledge expertise should be in the context of the problem that you are trying to solve. This means that you want to speak to the lawyer who actually sees the client's issue or is doing the pieces of work that the solution is aimed at. It is, more often than not, the people who are actually doing the work on a day-to-day basis who have the most useful insight. If the subject matter expert is not a partner, to make your life easier you will still want a partner aware of the project so that they can support the subject matter expert – either directly on the project or by freeing up their time.
- *Understands the client and market*. It is no good having an idea if the solution does not address a client's pain point, or they do not deem it worth paying for. Of course, there will be occasions where the innovation or product is seen as a "value add", but if you are looking to

productize some of your innovation efforts then this is unlikely to be sufficient for a sustainable strategy. If you have a more junior subject matter expert, they may need assistance with some of the wider market and pricing considerations – this is usually well worth the investment of time as, if they have spotted one issue, they are likely to spot more over the years and be amenable to working with you again.

- *Works well with others.* If you have a new subject matter expert on a project that you have not worked with before, it can be useful to get some informal views on them from people who have – how did they cope with change, can they problem solve, how are they with deadlines. Ideally you want someone who works well with others. If this has not been the case historically, there is an outside chance that could be down to the particular peculiarities of a previous project, or the people involved, but at least you have had some warning and can prepare accordingly.
- *Works well without a detailed plan.* In the context of starting an innovation project, there is a fine line between over-preparing and under-preparing – sometimes you just have to get started with an overall end point in mind and work out the details as you go. Sometimes, the lack of visibility may be because you are doing something new and will have to try a couple of different ways of solving the problem to see what works. Other times, you may be honing a process, which also requires some agility. Subject matter experts who need to know every detail before they start are likely to find this way of working particularly challenging but even with a relatively static process they should not need to know all the ins and outs. Breaking down your innovation process into broad stages, such as exploration, proof of concept, and so on, can help with their understanding and expectation setting.

Setting expectations

It is vital to set expectations with the subject matter expert from the start, and equally to hear what the subject matter expert is expecting themselves. Expectations from the subject matter experts are likely to be high; the expectations from an innovation and product perspective are likely to be more realistic (or at least aware of limitations and potential hurdles). Areas for potential misalignment between expectations include:

- *Time commitments.* You need to be sensitive to the pinch points within your firm at certain times of year,[2] which could be related to billing, promotion periods, or other projects that are unrelated to yours.

- *Required input.* Subject matter experts tend to significantly underestimate the amount of time a task will take them by at least 100 percent. This is no matter how much you try and set out the task and the time they have available. Whilst this can often be frustrating for an innovation team, you soon get used to giving out deadlines to subject matter experts that grant you a bit of slack and do not derail the overall project plan. The almost certain failure to meet a deadline does, however, let you juggle multiple other projects which, if everyone came back to you with their actions completed on time, you would not be able to do!
- *Project lifecycles.* Not only do subject matter experts often underestimate the amount of time their input into a project will take, they also significantly (and often to the same degree of magnitude) underestimate how quickly a project can be delivered. This is to be expected and is not a problem, provided that they have not told the client a delivery date that they have not first run past the innovation team. Explaining some of the high-level tasks that an innovation team will have to do without the involvement of the subject matter expert can help them understand some of the hidden work in a project – for example, Data Privacy Impact Assessments and testing.

Building trust by delivering

Subject matter experts can be skeptical that you can actually solve their client's problem (assuming your subject matter expert has got to the nub of the problem that needs solving). The only solution to this is to deliver the project. An award nomination is an added bonus; an award win, even better; an award win for a solution off the back of a client's endorsement, the best yet. When you have done this once for a subject matter expert, you will often find that they come back for additional projects – congratulations, you have them on side for life!

The importance of listening

Lawyers are usually the people in a room who are giving the advice. It can therefore be quite a shift for them to be in a room where they are not the expert (or certainly not the only expert). The good ones recognize the limits of their expertise and are more than happy to listen to the expertise of others. This is particularly important if you have a more junior innovation team, as you will spend time telling them that they have a right to be in a meeting with a roomful of senior lawyers and that they are there for their expertise. It is key to help them appreciate that they are the ones with knowledge about innovation in the room. Listening also requires the ability to ask a good question – Edgar Schein has written a really useful book on the topic of humble inquiry.[3]

Someone needs to be the translator

The mix of people on a project and in a meeting is important to the overall success of an innovation project. You are likely to have experts from multiple different domains involved ranging across law, software, computer science, process change, and everything in between. At first, everyone is trying to understand everyone else's language – the more you can avoid technical jargon and abbreviations the better. Even when that is done very successfully, there is still often a need to bridge the knowledge gap and act as a translator. This task often falls to the innovation team, who alongside having their own expertise, have picked up enough from other areas to be able to understand key concepts.

The concept of the "O" shaped lawyer[4] is popular at the moment; we would argue that the O shaped attributes and vision should apply equally to the other professionals who work in a law firm, especially product and innovation teams. Building on this, Adam Curphey promulgates that there are four areas of law+ skills, namely people, business, change, and tech, that are "plus" the law.[5] Within that, Curphey also explains that there are four different areas of mastery, ranging from entry level to expert, and one lawyer will not possess all the skills to the level of expert. Within a team or a project then you are looking for the mix of skills and mastery to be as balanced as you can. The more O shaped attributes the people on an innovation project have, the easier it is likely to be to work together and solve the problem effectively.

- *Works well with others.* The same considerations apply from the discussion above in the context of the right lawyer.
- *Ok with a destination even though the path to get there may not be 100 percent visible.* The same considerations apply from the discussion above in the context of the right lawyer. We have found that chunking the product and innovation process up has helped subject matter

experts understand more about the process. After all, everything is a process at some level.

Collaborating with lawyers – what does not work?

Unsurprisingly, what does not work is the opposite of what does. This includes:

Lack of time

When the subject matter expert cannot invest the time to work with the people who can help translate the idea into an MVP at least, you are unlikely to make any great progress. Lawyers typically like to work in periods of quarter, half, and year ends – the trouble is not everyone else does! This can make resource planning difficult and, in a worst-case scenario, has the potential to overwhelm an innovation team if everything spikes around the start of each quarter (when subject matter experts have time) and then fizzles out towards the end of the quarter (when lawyers' priorities change). From an innovation management perspective, we have found being a little firmer with deadlines and explaining that projects will lose their place in the queue or prioritization framework if we cannot secure their time when we need it helps to ease this a bit and, with each year, this has become less of an issue. In the early years, where you have more lulls in projects, this has been a good time to invest in upskilling, R&D, creating internal communications to schedule over the quarter, and refining your existing processes.

Reluctance to change

Often closely related to having a lack of time, sometimes there is a general reluctance to want to try doing things in a different way. The standard objection is usually along the lines of maintaining that the current process works and there is no spare time to change this and retrain. This may be so in the middle of delivering a specific client project, but if the same team keeps having the same issues when delivering particular types of work, then previous practices clearly do not continue to serve them well.

Of course, tensions may be running high during the delivery of a specific project, so change is often best not attempted then! What you can do at this stage is make sure you are documenting as many of the issues or requests as you can, so that after the project you can work with them to reimagine how the work may be delivered. This can often be achieved by a session that does a retrospective review of the issues, which then allows you to plan how they can be avoided or mitigated next time around. The retrospective needs to include views from all involved, especially those who actually did the tasks, so this could include admin, lawyers, data teams, and finance teams. Putting everyone in a room, virtual or otherwise, and asking what could be better may not achieve the desired result – people may not want to look like they are criticizing the process, for example.

What can help is having a mechanism in place whereby people can highlight the issues that arose and suggestions as to how to improve it. We have found virtual whiteboard collaboration platforms useful for this as they allow people to post, anonymously if they wish, their issues or ideas. It also means people can add to it at a time that suits them, and this is likely to be when they have a bit more time to be engaged with the issues, rather than being put on the spot at a brainstorming session. Depending on the project, you can divide the board up by different aspects of the project and even ask people to vote (again anonymously if required) on what is the most acute challenge to fix. This method of asynchronous collaboration often works well at ensuring those with more introvert preferences are involved and not silenced by the loudest in a room and especially not by the aforementioned HiPPO.

Believing in magic

Innovation is not magic. Getting something up and running from nothing requires a substantial amount of effort. There are some subject matter experts who think they just have to describe what they want and it will be delivered on a plate next week, perfectly formed as they imagined it (but did not actually describe it) without any further involvement on their part. The innovation process requires education across the firm about your processes and the value of the subject matter expert's involvement, rather than just lobbing something over the proverbial innovation wall and hoping for the best! This links back to the discussion above about needing to set expectations early on.

Sudden experts in everything

It can be difficult to admit you do not know something. Whilst in a legal context, a lawyer would not think twice about handing a task over to a colleague with a different specialism to their own, in an innovation context everybody seems to have an opinion on the best way of doing something and is more than prepared to have a go. Whilst you do not wish to curb any enthusiasm, you also do not want to get bogged down in exploring particularly random ideas that may or may not require stitching various spreadsheets together! One way that we have found to deal with this whilst maintaining levels of enthusiasm is to collect all the ideas as part of your exploration process so that they can then be presented back to the subject matter expert alongside a range of other (more viable) potential solutions. As we keep mentioning, innovation is a people game and part of this involves upskilling your colleagues on the types of solutions available so that, by the time they are on their second or third project with you, their suggestions are more in line with what you need. Much like painting the Forth Road Bridge, this is a never-ending cycle as technology is constantly evolving, so the ways of solving problems are also constantly evolving.

When being a lawyer goes to their head
Sometimes, lawyers cannot get out of lawyer mode. This can manifest itself in a few ways such as the lawyer thinking that only their way is correct, being defensive, and generally resistant to change. A fair amount of cajoling is usually required to kick them out of this and recognize that there are often multiple, equally right, ways of approaching the same problem. Sometimes you may just have to have a quiet word, or ask someone who has a bit more situational power to do so.

Tangentially related tasks
There are some people who, no matter how hard you plan, involve them, or keep them updated, are like magpies and become fixated on the most interesting or less important tasks. Quite often, this is due to those tasks being more familiar to them, so they are generally more comfortable adopting them. Whilst it may appear relatively harmless (at least they are engaged), you are likely to end up with scope creep, or the real tasks that will drive the project forward are avoided. Both mean that the project will at best end up delayed, or worst case will not be able to deliver what it was supposed to.

A total avoidance of risk
There are occasions where lawyers only want to innovate where someone has already done it before. Sometimes this is not a problem, but if there is a brilliant idea (that even hits all your prioritization criteria) there is nothing more likely to kill it than if a lawyer can only proceed after evidence of similar success. It usually pays dividends to try and explore where this reluctance comes from so that you can try to surmount it. It could be linked with a promotion, or simply a fear of trying something unfamiliar that they do not

want to fail. Positioning the project as a collective one where you succeed as a team can help allay some of this reluctance.

Working with clients – the moon on a stick

Clients are at the heart of everything law firms do, and these days most firms aspire to be something along the lines of a technology-driven, data-led, and innovative law firm. As we detailed in earlier chapters, one of the reasons for setting up an innovation team in the first place was as a result of client demand for innovation. Innovation teams love nothing better than seeing their solutions being used, and what better way to demonstrate an innovation team's worth to the rest of the business than by working with actual clients. In the early days of our innovation efforts, we found that innovation was often a useful hook to speak to clients – in particular their business service teams, which lawyers would rarely interact with. We are lucky that we continue to have numerous opportunities to speak and work with clients and have multiple innovations and products with clients in real life use, some of which are SaaS products that we license for a subscription fee.[6]

Whilst working with clients on innovation projects and products is exciting, it can give rise to issues (and opportunities!) that you may not have encountered in the more traditional arena of legal services. We have included a case study later in this section but there are many similarities with working with your own internal lawyers that we have discussed above. Some issues that may require handling a bit differently given the client angle are set out here.

Clients do not have time

This is unlikely to come as a surprise. Clients do not have an abundance of spare time, so how do you get to work with them on an innovation project? Granted, there are elements of serendipity about it, but you can increase your chances of this by understanding their problems and then approaching them to see if you can help solve them, which often then snowballs into a wider discussion. If you think of some of the best tech demos or approaches you have seen, they are generally more tailored to the areas of work your firm does, the types of clients you work with, or something that you have written or spoken about – some hook to draw you in rather than a generic approach. Whilst you do not want to presume you know all of the problems facing a client, you also do not want to know nothing about the area in which they operate. Often you can use a previous example of similar work as a hook to get a meeting with a client to show your understanding of the relevance. In practice, understanding your clients' problems can involve:

- Speaking with colleagues who work with the clients to find out what types of issues they are working on for the client. Have they got particular concerns about what is in their contracts, do they have regulatory concerns, is there a specific type of claim that they frequently face? What conversations have your colleagues had with the clients about their business? If you collect data relating to the matters on which you act for the clients, are there any patterns?
- Researching the client. What is on their website, do they have an annual report, what do their accounts show, have they been in the news, written articles, or spoken at events?
- General research into the client's industry – what is going on in the world that may affect them – is ESG important to them, what will be the impact of any political or legal reforms?
- Arguably a lot of this is marketing/sales table stakes but it remains surprising to hear GCs talk about their panel firms to the effect that a lot of this still doesn't happen universally.

Clients do not know what they do not know

It is hard to see an internal blind spot, but it is often easier from the outside. We mentioned using data to look for patterns in the work you do for a client, for example does looking at the data by branch or office show a variation in the volume or outcome of a particular type of claim? Is this down to people, process, or a combination? You will often need to work with your colleagues to hypothesize and add some context to the raw data. This is a good way of coming across potential areas on which to collaborate with clients – you can tell them something useful that they may not have known about their business, whilst at the same time suggesting a way of exploring a solution together.

Clients can struggle to articulate their issues or do not always tell you all their issues

Although this can happen in a legal context, it is also worth bearing in mind in an innovation context. As innovation is a people game, the art of asking a good question and really listening to the answer does not go amiss and is as important in the innovation context as it is in more traditional lawyer/client interactions. There is nothing wrong with having a checklist of topics to cover, or some problem-solving techniques jotted down so you do not forget anything during a discussion. The Five Whys technique[7] is an easy one to remember and can help to get to the root cause of an issue. Sometimes, you may need information outside the knowledge of the person you are talking to – this is often the case if IT, HR, or risk involvement is required. After an exploratory session it is often useful to involve a wider selection of people from the client, or contact them with a precis of the project, to ask if they foresee any issues or if they have any requirements, for example around roll-out timings (HR), multi-factor authentication (IT), or the data in a specific region (risk) – all very useful to know.

Clients' legal departments have their own demands and priorities

If you have ever been involved in procuring external software or services in your organization then this may be familiar – expect clients' legal, IT, and risk departments to be involved, which can slow down progress. Again, visibility of this at the start of a project is useful and can help you plan and anticipate any hurdles and take steps to mitigate them, including making sure deadlines build in any required approval time (and avoid busy periods for the client team). You may also need to fill in information security and other pre-qualification questionnaires if you are suppling a technological-based solution, which means you are likely to have to liaise with your own risk team too. All of this can significantly elongate the project lifecycle.

Clients do not often get much time from their IT teams

If you are dealing with a legal team at a client, they often receive the bare minimum from their IT department, who are often focused on supporting the rest of the client's service delivery. This can be a challenge or an opportunity, depending upon your project! If your solution needs to integrate with a client's system, then the lack of IT resource can hamper your project, but if you are delivering a cloud solution then IT departments are often very welcoming as they know they will not have to do much to support the project.

On client-facing projects you will need a plan for general queries such as problems logging on or password reminders. We have always signposted our queries inbox to the client's IT team so they can forward queries to us and we also detail how to contact us as part of our overall roll-out. We have found the easiest way to manage in practice is for the innovation team to have a shared inbox to deal with this type of query.

Case study: Decision support tool – Equality Act 2010

Challenge/opportunity

Our lawyers analyzed claims data for a FTSE100 client with 10,000 HR managers and were able to understand where and why their main type of employment tribunal liability arose – disability discrimination. The client wants to treat people properly and fairly and the Act prescribes how to do this, both procedurally and substantively. The challenge for the client was that being able to actually demonstrate that it had treated its employees fairly was quite technical and not something an individual manager did frequently enough to be familiar with. As a consequence, it was easy to make mistakes and misapply the Act's provisions, which is distressing for the individuals involved and costly for the organization.

Strategy

We developed a decision-making software tool to help our client improve the consistency of decision-making in disability discrimination claims to better ensure that they were treating their employees fairly, in terms of both running the process and the ultimate decision. The innovation team worked with our expert lawyers and end users (HR managers) at the client to deliver this project. We delivered the tool, as well as communications for the client to inform users of the new tool and how to use it.

The software tool guides HR managers through the decision-making process and is tailored to the specific client, including referencing its own internal guidance. It uses responses provided by the HR managers to questions so that it can:

- Assist clients with understanding the legal test for disability;
- Enable clients to identify the relevant issues and reach an informed decision as to whether an employee is likely to be classed as disabled or not; and
- Assist clients with having open discussions with employees regarding medical conditions/disabilities and create a record of the individual's circumstances that can form part of a disability-type passport.

The tool documents the decision-making process and emails the outcome report to the user, making it auditable and transparent, evidencing the information that has affected the decision. The success of this project has spawned further requests from the same client who now has multiple tools in use. It has also led to the development of a tool to assist with the next stage of the process, which covers making reasonable adjustments.

People – the importance of involving them in the execution

The innovation team worked remotely with the client's legal and HR teams, their project management team, and our expert lawyers to unpack decision-making around disability discrimination. After scoping meetings, our legal engineers were able to create numerous process maps and question flows which were then built into an MVP demo tool in a no code platform. A prototype was important at this stage so that our lawyers could see how the tool question flow would work for the ultimate end user prior to demonstration. This was a collaborative and agile process between the innovation team and expert lawyers who were then able to validate the MVP tool so it could be demonstrated to the client. The tool development was an iterative process to ensure it would be as user friendly as possible. Feedback during the pilot was invaluable for this and resulted in amendments. The tool was seamlessly launched to 10,000 HR managers in December 2021.

We used a no code platform as we wanted to provide a secure self-serve technological solution at scale for use across thousands of managers. We needed a way of ensuring that answering questions in the same way would produce a consistent answer; the platform allowed us to do this, and without needing IT team resource for changes and tweaks. We also wanted to ensure the user interface and operation of the system was simple and intuitive for the users and would not require training sessions to be able to operate it. We also wanted to be able to segregate the data so we could report on how many times the tool is run, without us having access to the underlying data inputted.

Excellent senior-level buy-in from the client helped with the design process and provided an initial pilot group. The solution is embedded into the client's HR system and their project team worked with us to ensure it fitted into their workflow. This allowed us to collaborate and ensure the tool met the client's needs, for example providing client-specific handoffs in the process.

We wanted to minimize queries to the client's HR or IT departments so included tooltips and guidance. The tool does not just provide an answer, it provides guidance on the things that the user should be finding out and considering. The question flows are conditional, so information is collected in sequence and if a user has not completed an important step (e.g., meeting with the colleague to discuss their disability) then the solution forces them to do this step before making a decision.

Outcome

The use of the tool begins to establish evidence and provide decision-making support. It also has the benefit of upskilling its users, both in the mechanics and composite parts of the test for disability; thereby not only improving the decision-making process for the case in hand, but also for any future cases that may then arise. Over time, the client will be able to demonstrate they have treated their employees fairly as their policies are now applied consistently and evidenced.

Implementation has been very successful. Since roll-out in December 2021, there have been over 3,000 outcome reports created, advising HR managers as to whether an employee is likely to be classed as disabled or not. This is over 3,000 occasions that historically gave rise for the potential for discrimination. In addition, the tool has been run over an additional 3,500 times, indicating that it is prompting managers to follow the full process by completing any missing steps (such as speaking to the colleague to discuss their disability) and by people keen to explore the new system.

What did we learn?

1. *Working at scale*. This is a good example of a solution where technology can help – which is to enable and evidence a repeatable and predictable process, at scale, cost effectively. It provided a solution that would not have been achievable if it required the HR manager to seek legal advice every time the issue arose.
2. *Success breeds opportunities*. Engaging with the client has meant they have asked us to work with them to develop further tools based specifically on their processes, which, had we not been involved in the original tool, we would not have been asked to do.
3. *Understanding innovation capabilities is key*. Really understanding a client's business can lead to solutions where our subject matter expert lawyer understood the capabilities of the innovation team. The client would never have asked their lawyers for an app to help them ensure they treated their employees fairly under the Act.

Working with external suppliers

Stuart had an experience as a lawyer where his client was more difficult to deal with than the opponent – the client was not getting the best out of him as a lawyer, and it was quite a hostile relationship. When Stuart moved into the IT department, more than 20 years ago, similarly combative relationships existed with core suppliers, making for unpleasant meetings all round. Recognizing from his previous experience that this was not getting the best out of anyone, Stuart turned this around to create symbiotic relationships with suppliers. This approach has really shaped our thinking and interactions with external technology and innovation suppliers. We will sit through any tech demo that interests us or we can see potential in and foster relationships and networks that might not result in procuring the technology for a couple of years (until a use case comes up or a start-up has developed their product). That strength of relationship means that any pilots and procurement are straightforward – we told you innovation is a people game!

Software suppliers need customers who are willing to work with them in the same way innovation teams need clients willing to work with them. By adopting this approach, we are able to see technology roadmaps and help shape them, co-present at conferences, undertake joint awards nominations, discuss use cases as part of client advisory boards, and get advance access to new features. Whilst this comes at a time cost to us as an organization, the benefit of building deeper and more connected relationships with our suppliers outweighs this and enables conversations with all areas of our suppliers' businesses, not just those focused on sales or customer success.

Working with other law firms

We have both had far more collaborative discussions with our innovation peers in other firms than either of us ever had as a lawyer. Perhaps this is because innovation leaders often have the ability to lead through uncertainty and ambiguity, take action, and create structures in chaos – a collection of skills known as the chaos pilot.[8] This can be quite a lonely role, so those of us tasked with leading innovation welcome the ability to connect with our peers to discuss what is working and what is not and share war stories – this is often very helpful, and a lot of those conversations have informed this book. It is perfectly possible to not share any trade secrets but still have a meaningful decision with peers from other firms. The more you talk, the more that you realize we are all largely facing the same series of problems, often around common topics such as people, time, money, and change management. This seems to be a universal truth regardless of the size of the firm or the area of law that they operate in.

Working with academia – is there a disconnect between research and reality?

We have always enjoyed our projects with academia and welcomed the different approach, opportunities, and perspective they have provided us with. There are certainly some tips and tricks we have learnt from these collaborations that make life easier for everyone, and we explore them in the following case study.

Case study: Decision support – turning academic ideas into practical tools

Challenge/opportunity

We wanted to explore if advances in computer science meant that we could build tools that would support lawyers to make decisions, for example determining liability in tortious actions. The idea was to build software that would mimic a lawyer's mental reasoning and see if we could tie this in with data extraction to help populate the answers to some of the questions.

We spent two years collaborating on a particular use case – knowledge sharing and undertaking experimentation. Our work with the University of Liverpool, a document review software company, and a no code platform allowed us to turn business ideas and academic research into reality, developing an AI solution able to extract data to power a decision engine capable of carrying out legal reasoning in a particular domain.

Strategy

Our approach to innovation has been to augment rather than replace lawyers and we foresee a symbiotic relationship. Accordingly, success for us with legal AI was to allow our lawyers to focus only on those elements of the work that require proper, formal, legal input, minimizing their time on more mundane and repetitive tasks and adding real value to clients as a result.

We used personal injury claims as the testing ground for some of our AI and technology activities in order to understand where we can derive benefit from the various approaches for our clients. This is in part driven by our experience that there are elements of those claims that are repeatable and predictable, and it is work that the firm undertakes at scale so, in theory, ought to be suitable to test out ideas.

It is important to us that we solve specific real-world issues, creating bespoke solutions for the needs of our clients and colleagues, rather than off-the-shelf products. We are not looking to utilize technology for the sake of it and the firm's innovation plan has been grounded in academic theory for this exact reason.

People

The concept of collaboration is at the heart of our approach to innovation. This has seen us focus on how people – together with co-bots, not robots – can drive innovation and intelligent working. Our legal experts collaborated with renowned academics to understand how computer systems can engage in the process of reasoning in the legal arena, with everyone deriving valuable insights into the logic behind the legal process. However, legal reasoning is just one aspect of our collaborative approach; legal claims produce large volumes of unstructured data, and utilizing the document review software allowed us to bring structure to this. This in turn allowed us to power a decision engine built in-house that is capable of carrying out legal reasoning.

Execution

We worked with the University of Liverpool's head of computer science, Professor Katie Atkinson, and the late Professor Trevor Bench-Capon (renowned global experts on AI and law) on the project.

We combined our framework with document review software that provides the data extraction capabilities required for a decision engine. The software automatically identifies and extracts material metadata into an exportable summary, which is then fed into the decision engine to assist with decision-making and argument identification. Until our work with this particular document review software, it had not been used on personal injury claims, so our own experts trained and refined its machine learning capabilities. Insurance claims was not a use case that was contemplated by the vendor but which the vendor made possible by virtue of the machine learning element of the product that allowed us to train it on novel documents.

In conjunction with the University of Liverpool, a peer reviewed paper on our approach was presented at the 30th International Conference on Legal Knowledge and Information Systems in Luxembourg, and further papers followed.

Outcome

Rather than simply developing a series of different, single-point solutions for various use cases, we used the in-depth understanding provided by integration with the University of Liverpool to establish an adaptable tool that could be easily adopted and speed up a time-intensive process for lawyers.

What did we learn?

- *Listening is very important.* Do not presuppose you know the problem to be solved or how the end user wants to interact with a solution. Listen (and iterate). It can require a shift in mindset to be the one being advised on options or different ways of doing things. This is even more so with academia. Pick collaborators that you can get on with and work with.
- *Drivers.* The drivers of businesses and universities are often very different. Universities are focused on high-scoring research and publications to satisfy the Research Excellence Framework (which feeds the university ranking list), as well as sometimes exploring areas out of interest. This means a focus on peer-reviewed journal articles and academic conferences. For law firms, the focus is on getting something real and tangible that can be used to improve turnaround, cost, consistency of decision making, or an innovation project involving a client.
- *Calendars.* Be realistic from the start on how much time each collaborator has available and needs. Synchronize calendars so you know when you will be short on availability of key people (for university this is start of terms, exams, and conference season; for law firms this is quarter, half, and year ends).
- *Translation.* If you think a roomful of lawyers is hard to manage, try a roomful of lawyers and academics! The mix of people in the room is important. At first everyone is still trying to understand everyone's language (e.g., software, computer science, law) – someone needs to act as a translator so that people can begin to understand each other from the start.

Working with funding bodies – dealing with life at a different pace

We have been fortunate enough to win external funding on several occasions, which has allowed us to work on projects and ideas that otherwise we would not have had the expertise or people to commit to. Quite often, these applications are made in conjunction with academic institutions, so the discussion in relation to working with academia equally applies here. Whilst extra funding and resource is always to be welcomed, there are some particular quirks of external funding that need a bit of thought.

- *Be mindful of timescales.* The time from application to getting started can vary massively depending upon the sort of external funding you bid for. We have had decisions within six months and nearly 12 months, bringing the total time from preparing the application to starting the project to approximately 18 months – usually, the competition for funding is only live for a matter of weeks. The questions often have short (500-1,000) word limits to cover substantial topics and there is a real skill to writing this kind of document succinctly, especially if the application involves multiple parties. Word limits and document size limits are absolute – ignore them at your peril or you will find that you cannot enter any more text in the box and that your application is stopped mid-sentence or you cannot get the crucial project plan to upload. Strong project management skills are definitely called for. We may have been just unlucky, but deadlines often correspond with traditional holiday times, which all adds to the stress of getting everything submitted on time!
- *Picking the right project.* As a result of elongated timescales, picking a project can prove tricky. The project needs to be something substantial enough that it warrants external funding, but also something that you can wait 18 months to get started on (costs incurred on a project prior to a funding award as a general rule are not recoverable). We have tended to pick ideas that are outside the scope of our technical or resource limitations but where there is enough academic research to show that it might be possible to put into practice, or which would otherwise take 100 percent of our resource.
- *Think of the audience.* Many funding assessors are very used to assessing applications written by academics. There is a whole industry that has arisen around drafting funding applications and even the most technical lawyer tends not to write like an academic. Given the

tight word limits, it is hard to get the balance right between business and academic. You need to imagine your marker is an educated expert, but not necessarily in the exact topic of your application or with any business background. Much like math homework, showing your reasoning is important – you should not assume that anything focused on law firms as a business will be known to the markers. You need to remove jargon, make your answers clear to understand, and explicitly answer the question presented.

- *Project management*. If the funding is from a research council or similar, then deviation from the submitted plan is only allowed if this has been agreed by the funding body or the monitoring officer who works on their behalf. Meetings with the monitoring officer occur at regular intervals and are an opportunity to present on current progress, any barriers, and any changes required. Although they are unlikely to have domain knowledge, they bring a wealth of experience of collaboration and project management and often provide suggestions that you can apply in your other projects.

Working with micro and start-up businesses

Whilst many companies you end up working for are well established, there may be times when you work with a micro company, perhaps if they are undertaking some cutting-edge work that you want to be involved in. This can be really exciting as often the project is their full focus and they are agile and keen to work with you. The flip side of this is a number of potential risks, including the ability to complete a project – for example, what happens if a key employee leaves. There can also be challenges around their systems and policies, which may be untested or not even exist, which will pose challenges for your supply management/procurement colleagues. You may be the biggest firm that the start-up has worked with, and they are likely not used to requests for their anti-bribery or Modern Slavery Act policies as, with two employees, it was not top of their list of priorities. There have been occasions where we have provided example policies so that a micro company can develop their own and thereby satisfy our supplier-management processes. In this type of relationship, it is even more imperative to involve your risk and procurement colleagues early in the discussions.

Chapter checklist

- ☐ Do you have a good understanding of how your legal and business service teams work and what business as usual is for them?
- ☐ Can you identify colleagues that display innovative qualities?
- ☐ Do you understand your clients' world? If not, who can help you?
- ☐ Do you have any existing relationships with academia that you could build upon?
- ☐ How can you learn more about your existing suppliers and what else they may be able to help you with?

References

1 See chapter six – the "Gold dust lawyer".

2 See chapter three, for example, which includes some of the times to best avoid a pilot.

3 Schein, E., and Schein, P., *Humble Inquiry: The Gentle Art of Asking Instead of Telling (second edition)* San Francisco: Berrett-Koehler Publishers, 2021.

4 The five Os are open, original, opportunity, ownership, and optimism. See: https://oshaped.com/.

5 Curphey, A., *The Legal Team of the Future: Law+ Skills*, London: London Publishing Partnership, 2022.

6 See: www.weightmans.com/products/transport-manager-comply/; www.weightmans.com/products/disability-tools/

7 As the name suggests, this technique involves asking why after each piece of information to move from the obvious symptoms to the root cause. For example, in relation to a slip in a supermarket the issue is not training on tomatoes – sorting the tomatoes does not prevent a similar incident with carrots, whereas training on shelf stacking would:

1. *Why did the person slip?*
   a. There was a spillage on the floor.
2. *Why was there a spillage on the floor?*
   a. The tomatoes had rolled off the shelf.
3. *Why had the tomatoes rolled off the shelf?*
   a. The tomatoes had rolled off the shelf as the shelf had been over stacked.
4. *Why had the shelf been over stacked?*
   a. The employee had not been trained on shelf stacking.
5. *Why had the employee not been trained on shelf stacking?*
   a. The employee had not been trained on shelf stacking as this was a mandatory new starter course but only ran once a quarter. [etc. you get the gist]

8 Furr, N., Nel, K., and Zoëga Ramsøy, T., "If Your Innovation Effort Isn't Working, Look at Who's on the Team", November 2018. See: https://hbr.org/2018/11/if-your-innovation-effort-isnt-working-look-at-whos-on-the-team.

Chapter 8: When things go wrong – bouncing back from lessons learned

We have failed at a lot of things along the way. They've not always been in a spectacular manner; sometimes just on specific technical- or people-related aspects of a project. Ideally, we like to fail fast, if that is not too trite a statement these days (we do, of course, prefer to succeed quickly). We always like to learn from failure and have a relaxed attitude to it as an opportunity to learn – we take the view that if we are not failing, we are not experimenting enough. Whilst within an innovation team this is an acceptable attitude to have, it is one that is truly alien within a law firm, given the general personality traits of lawyers. This shift in mindset can be difficult. In this chapter, we outline some of the types of failures we have had along the way and what we have learned from them.

Solving the wrong problem

Despite the best intentions of those involved, on several occasions people have attempted to solve the wrong problem. Sometimes serendipity has given us a chance to intervene as there will be many we have missed!

Solution knowledge gaps

Following the COVID-19 pandemic there was a shortage of HGV drivers in the UK, and one of our partners spotted a way of using existing immigration procedures to solve this problem. However, it required a fair amount of form filling and checking against a set of strict criteria. Based on their own experience, the partner thought the solution was a large number of paralegals filling in forms for clients. Faced with this, the partner was understandably panicking about how to recruit and manage an army of paralegals and develop workflows to deal with the processes.

We learned what was going on by accident and thought the process sounded consistent, scalable, and repeatable so there was likely to be a technology-based solution that could do some of the heavy lifting and prevent unnecessary recruitment. We managed to get stakeholders in a room before job adverts went out and, in the discovery workshop, we were able to get the lawyers to properly articulate the problem. The outcome was a client-based app that triaged potential HGV drivers by whether they satisfied the applicable immigration requirements.

The common denominator is the knowledge gap ("You don't know what you don't know"). The problem here was that the lawyer did not consider an alternative solution as they did not know what that might be, and they did not involve the right people in discussions early on. In order to attempt to mitigate this, internal profile raising of the innovation team's abilities can help, so that people have you front and center of their mind if they are trying to solve a problem. That said, you can do all the internal profile raising you like; lawyers typically only tend to look above their legal parapet when they need to, so this is a constant struggle. Sharing examples where you have helped a particular team do something for a client is a good way of getting some more interaction with this.

People are, unsurprisingly, often at the root of failure. Workflow and automation, indeed technology generally, will not solve people and process problems. If you are not managing your people to a standard way of working or do not actually have a standard way of working then technology will not solve that problem. All you get by throwing technology at a people and process problem is faster and more efficient chaos, so it is vital that you start with people and process before going anywhere near technology.

Solving a symptom and not a root cause

There is a tendency to look at technology as a panacea. The problem with adopting this approach is that it does not inherently solve problems and you will probably end up with a frustrated user when the technology cannot address their actual problem, as well as a load of (potentially expensive) shelfware. It is also likely to be a slow process, with various procurement hoops to jump through to secure the tech. There is often a much more low-tech way of quickly exploring a problem, which can enable you to get some more insight or (ideally) some actual, quantifiable data to help assess it. For example, if you want to see if everyone is doing their daily, weekly, or monthly tasks, there is little point saying that you won't do anything until you have a system. In that scenario, a starting point could be just a piece of paper and see how you get on, learning some lessons from working that way and discovering what you actually need. If the solution does transpire to be a technological one, you are in a much better position as you understand what you need, we all as, importantly, what you do not.

The "five whys" mentioned in chapter seven is a useful technique to help you get to the root cause of a problem, rather than a symptom of it. You start by asking why a particular problem happens and then continue to ask "Why?" until you get to the bottom of the problem. If the answer is "I don't know" then you are probably starting to get to a root cause. It is important to remember that there may be more than one root cause: training, management, and standardization are often elements of the root causes of underlying problems. Five times was chosen based on anecdotal evidence, so do not worry if you are not at exactly five whys.

In a process context, we had a particular area of work where we were not meeting the requirements to respond in a particular time period as set out in a client's SLA, and on first blush you might have been forgiven for thinking that the reason for that was because there weren't enough case handlers to service the work and thus to solve the problem we would need to recruit more people. We used the five whys approach to discover the root cause. What transpired was that, during part of the workflow there was a hand off to an admin person to do a 30-second job that historically was not considered cost effective for a lawyer to do. By the time the admin person handed the file back to the case handler (because the file went to the bottom of their large pile as they worked in chronological order), the SLA had been breached on half of the matters. By tweaking the process so that the case handler did the task instead, the issue was solved. Ironically, it probably took more than 30 seconds for the case handler to ask the admin colleague to do the task, so it was one of those situations where it was definitely easier to do the task yourself rather than delegate and slavishly follow a principle of having the right sort of work being done by the right sort of person!

Seduced by the art of the possible

The prospect of using IBM Watson for legal falls into this category. IBM Watson is a system that can answer questions that have been asked in natural language (long before the advent of the modern day LLM; it even took part in *Jeopardy!*, a popular American quiz show, and won – a whole other story). IBM took large volumes of information (at a capacity no single human being could ever keep on top of), such as the latest studies and approaches to illnesses and then selected those relevant to the particular patient's symptoms. At the time, the thought process was that if you looked at what IBM was doing in healthcare, that sounded a lot like what lawyers do – taking large volumes of legislation and precedent and applying them to the facts of the issue before them.[1] When we looked to see whether we could use Watson in this context, we realized that it was never going to work, or at least not for a cost that would make it remotely economical – indeed, even the healthcare applications have not been plain sailing.[2]

If we are honest, we started our decision support tools project[3] because we were seduced by the art of the possible. We had read the academic articles and could both envision the ultimate tool that would help lawyers to make decisions. Our problem was that both the academics and we had similarly grand visions, so neither of us kept the other in check in terms of scope. It was our first big project and there was even more about innovation that we did not know then, compared to now. If we were starting this project today, we would spend more time planning and defining the scope of an MVP and planning iterative releases. We took on the whole legal framework for areas such as liability in noise-induced hearing loss claims, rather than breaking it down for discrete releases that might have dealt with liability, causation, contributory negligence, and similar, which could have been tested individually and then joined together.

Boiling the ocean

We knew early on that to aid the user experience and prevent people having to type the same data between systems, we would need to build something in the background that could do this. We ended up with Decision and Navigation (DAN), which acts like a concierge in the background between various systems, such as a CMS, document review, and decision support platforms, passing data between them and ultimately back into a CMS and a data warehouse. This bit of middleware could not be bought off the shelf economically at the time and had to be developed in-house by our excellent developers. However, this took us several years as there were always other projects that trumped it in terms of prioritization and initially we tried to solve for all potential use cases rather than building the integrations a stage at a time.

We got really excited in relation to the decision support tools project in terms of using the tool to identify the least amount of information needed to make a decision depending upon which path had been chosen. We could foresee a lawyer answering a couple of questions when they first looked at a matter and then have the tool work out, based on the available information and knowing what was missing, the quickest way for the case handler to get the information needed to make a decision on liability, for example. What we were trying to reduce was the need for case handlers to gather evidence and answers to questions that would, in the scheme of things, be irrelevant as there was a path with fewer steps that could be used to get to the decision. This was all whilst maintaining explainability – we did not want a black box solution where no one could work out where the outcomes were coming from – scalability, repeatability, and explainability were at the forefront of our minds. At the time, there were too many potential permutations and combinations to realistically calculate the optimum pathway through the decision tree with the fewest next steps.

Case study: RPA and software assisted file opening

Challenge/opportunity

We previously abandoned file opening when the project was about 60 percent of the way through, due to scope creep and other projects being prioritized above it. We had another go at it a couple of years later, but this time took a different approach. We redesigned our file opening process using machine learning and robotic process automation (RPA) technology to substantially reduce the time taken on this previously manual process. The innovation in this initiative lay in the non-traditional use of the document review software, and bringing it together with disparate technologies such as a CMS and RPA. Working with our CMS ensured that the user experience was positive, seamlessly joining up the different processes into an intuitive user interface and combining other, previously manual processes within it, such as conflict checking.

This initiative let technology do the heavy lifting to open clients' files faster and reduced a lot of repetitive (and boring) effort. The solution was built in a scalable way so it could be reused in other areas.

Strategy

The firm undertakes volume work for plot sales transactions. Instructed by electronic documents, we act on behalf of a housing developer who is selling new-build homes. This mechanism of instruction is common firm-wide in other legal areas. We open a file on our CMS to manage the transaction and, amongst other things, ensure compliance with regulatory requirements. This requires someone in an administrative role to open the matter on our CMS and then transcribe data and contact details (i.e., type in manually) from the client's PDF into our CMS.

The average time to open and set up the file manually was 64 minutes. For one client alone, we spent 486 hours a year opening files. Instruction levels vary seasonally, meaning the admin team can be overwhelmed. Being able to open files more quickly would allow us to progress the transactions and start working on them earlier. Given the time it takes to open a file manually, we also kept the data fields captured to a minimum. A more technological solution would allow us to capture additional data fields without any impact on the time taken to open the file. This could include data that could then be visualized to provide additional insights for the client. For example, Sales Agent A always adds a carpet with the sale, whereas Sales Agent B always adds a car charging point and ultimately gets a higher purchase price. This kind of insight is invaluable for clients, especially if they do not need to trawl through vast spreadsheets to work it out themselves. We decided to try a pilot with one plot sales client, with the modest aim to reduce the amount of time taken by 20 percent to 51 minutes.

We strongly believe that end users should be considered at every stage of the process from idea through to roll-out. From ideation to creation, we regularly sought feedback from the end users and made sure that any concerns were addressed, and recommendations were implemented.

People

From the beginning, we benefited from excellent senior leadership engagement. Our head of real estate and board took a keen interest in the development, implementation, and success of the project and was regularly provided with updates. Crucially, we had strong support from the plot sales team manager who ensured that end users were involved in the project, with input regularly sought and the technology developments played back to them. Drawing in all those involved in the process, from end-user to Board members, no doubt ensured a high level of user and manager buy-in for the process.

The plot sales team received training and support throughout the pilot, in both the new technology and their existing process to ensure that the different stages of the operation worked symbiotically, and all tools were utilized to their full potential. A SOP document was provided to users and individual training was conducted, which had a huge influence in the first few weeks of going live as they could ask whatever questions they liked and rerun the process as many times as they needed until they were comfortable using it.

Execution

The innovation team ran a series of ideation workshops, collaborating with our developer, case management workflow, legal, and administrative teams in order to better understand and unpack the process firsthand. We focused on reducing the time spent manually entering data. We successfully trained the document review software on the information contained in the instruction forms. Given the plethora of regulatory requirements to which we were subject, and the significance of file opening and conflict checks to enable us to comply with those requirements, we involved our risk and compliance team at the earliest opportunity to get their agreement in principle to our proposed approach.

We mapped out the new processes, which at a high level comprised:

- Upload to the document review software;
- Data extraction;
- Data download;
- Contact matching (e.g., matching people and names and addresses with data already held in our CMS);
- Management information insertion into the CMS; and
- Mapping – allowing the user to configure the mapping between the document review template and CMS.

We determined that an RPA solution would be able to assist with the physical opening of the file and data insertion, overlaid by a screen built by our developers to validate the data being used. Our workflow and developer colleagues built the RPA mechanism to ingest the data and input it into our CMS via a user interface. The second stage of the process allowed the user to double-check any inputted data, link any required associates (contacts) to the file, and view where the data had been pulled from (so they could satisfy themselves that the software had extracted the relevant bit of information) – taking an augmented approach to innovation to reduce the risk of any incorrect data being used. With the file then open in our CMS and the data fields automatically inserted, we then set about to use this to trigger an automatic conflict search, further reducing the manual data-entry time required.

Outcome

This project greatly exceeded our initial expectations and goals. In total, we were able to reduce the average time to open a file to 35 minutes (an impressive 45 percent reduction). When scaled up to all plot sales instructions for our pilot client, we will have reduced the time taken to open them from 1,813 hours/52 weeks to 992 hours/28 weeks. We clearly validated the proof of concept and with increased document automation this time can be reduced even further. We can open files in bulk (new functionality) and have reduced the need to employ people seasonally to cope with variable volume of files. The time saving means our colleagues can undertake more varied work. In addition, we have increased the type of data we can collect on instruction. As this data builds, we can visually display this to the client via dashboards, demonstrating our ability to not only process the data but provide valuable insights into outcomes and what this data really means for our clients.

This project was a proof of concept for one client in one area; we knew it if worked it would have firm-wide significance as we open thousands of files a year where the technology could be used either to open files in bulk or to speed up a heavily manual process. The proof of concept therefore proceeded with this in mind and has been built in a scalable way so that the solution can be reused in other areas and on other clients, such as a standard way for requesting file opening fields for the software. The project has also sparked conversations with other teams, for example those servicing client helplines, as to how we can quickly automate file opening for them.

What did we learn?

- *Involving users from the beginning helps with buy-in.* It is always great to have access to end users throughout the life of a project as it helps with the ultimate roll-out. A balance needs to be struck between keeping them informed and seeking their input, and a state of paralysis where nothing is done without recourse to them. Regular meetings where the latest iteration of a solution is shown to the end users and their feedback sought is a useful way of keeping projects going and not wasting development time on a fully formed solution that is not really what they need. You also need to make sure that you have a broad sample of end users involved; you do not want to end up making a solution that only suits the peculiarities of one end user.
- *Throwing the baby out with the bathwater.* No matter how tempting it is to start a project from scratch when you pick up something that has been tried before, it is always worth picking over the bones of the

previous attempt. It may be that there are bits that can be recycled, or lessons learned from things that had been tried previously.

- *Picking up a half-complete project requires a clear vision to sell it.* Buy-in is even more important if you are trying something that has already been explored. When you are starting the project, it is important to set the scene so that the team knows it can use the old work (with a constructive eye) and that the aim is to solve the problem, not to assign blame.

Being swayed by the loudest voice

There are two potential traps if you act on things as a result of being swayed by the loudest voice.

- *The voice is reflective of an extreme position rather than a consensus.* For example, if you are asking users for feedback, you do not want to act on the basis of one voice and go down one development path rather than another. One way of getting around this is to not make all the feedback a group discussion where the loudest voice carries sway, which means that others may not wish to express a counter view, especially if the loudest voice is from one of the most senior people in the room (the HiPPO). Other ways of getting feedback include survey forms or online virtual collaboration platforms where people can leave (anonymous if they wish) feedback. In terms of deciding a features roadmap where there are conflicting views, it can often help to allocate everyone a fictional amount of money, for example 100 pounds, and ask them to place as much as they would like next to each feature. This seems to work better than just asking people to rank features in order of importance as you get a better sense of the scale of the importance of the feature – there is nothing stopping someone putting 90 pounds on one thing and then a couple of pounds on some of the others.
- *The "wrong" things get worked on.* Through necessity, we have honed our prioritization process[4] over the years and are now much better at pushing back so that more thought gets put into them before the commencement of any project. However, there are still occasions where things slip through when the argument in terms of urgency and demand is convincing.

Client tenders are a particular pinch point that can result in you being swayed by the loudest voice. The request, usually from a partner, is to build a solution for a specific tender in a tight timeline; the partner usually then plays the law firm trump card suggesting that there is a risk that the client could be lost without it. Unfortunately, even if you deliver this solution, the danger is that the partner in question may lose interest in it rapidly after the tender process has ended (that is, until the next tender when they ask how the solution has progressed).

The loudest voice can also result in the substantive work not getting started, for example if a lawyer says we need a website, some collateral, and a video before the solution or product can involve the clients. Often, the lack of these things is used as a justification for a lack of progress when in reality the lawyers just need to understand their product and go out and do the hard yards, wearing out the shoe leather, real or virtual. That said, we have become adept at spinning these things up really quickly to remove any barriers, real or perceived, to getting on with the selling.

The wisdom of crowds or following like lemmings?

There are solutions that many involved in innovation in law firms can see are used simply because everyone else uses them. This is often despite there being better and more commercially attractive alternatives available, and the existing solution being comparatively slow to iterate and develop new features. Usually this is driven by familiarity from previous jobs, and the knowledge that, if challenged, we can point to other (bigger?) firms who use the same solution. The path of least resistance is usually adopted rather than going back to basics and talking to the client about what they are actually trying to achieve (assuming, of course, that the client is open to that sort of conversation). Some of the solutions have been around for a long time and the thought of having to migrate things into another platform can seem overwhelming.

Sometimes, solutions can be chosen just so that the voices asking, *"What are you doing about innovation?"* or *"What are you doing about AI?"*, can be silenced in that area. The problem with this approach is that it rarely silences them – they just move on to requesting something else (and don't use the thing that you have just bought that there was supposedly such an urgent need for). This cycle of purchasing to silence continues, along with the accumulation of shelfware. A better approach is to stand firm and work with the people making the requests to understand the problem that they are trying to solve – to which they believe they have identified a solution already – and help them solve it (a theme that will have become familiar to you during the course of reading this book). On occasion, you will find there was not even a problem that needed solving and that you were just the metaphorical punch bag. A particularly amusing exchange that we will leave you to guess how exaggerated for effect it is went:

Partner: *"I see firm X has a solution for [insert really niche area of work]. We are falling behind, we need to have one too."*

Innovation: *"Ok, let's take a look – what is the revenue for this niche area of work, how many people do it, is it a growing area of work for the relevant segment?"*

Partner: *"Oh, we don't do the niche area of work [or in fact anything like it] but firm X has a solution and we are falling behind."*

Innovation: *"Er, ok – so we don't do the niche area of law. Let's look at the functionality of the solution they have created [e.g. it involves a risk assessment, triage, or document automation etc.]. Have we got any problems that the functionality could help solve?"*

Partner: *"Don't be daft. We just need the same solution as firm X."*

Innovation: *[Whilst banging head against a wall] "Well, we are always happy to speak to clients and solve actual problems, we don't tend to do too well with clients the problems of which nobody knows anything about (including the client)!"*

Assuming the end user knows what they want

All law firms have software solutions that they have bought and delivered, and the very people who asked for it do not use because it was not what they thought they were getting. This ties back into the lemmings example above and ends up being frustrating for everyone involved. On occasion, the situation is salvageable by starting again with the software (much to the frustration of the users, which requires some deft stakeholder management) and working out what problem they thought it was solving and then seeing if it is possible to fit this imperfect solution to the actual problem, whilst reframing and resetting expectations.

Sometimes it is not just about the end user. Sometimes the organization needs to impose requirements on end users, regardless of what they want to do, for perfectly sensible and reasonable organizational reasons. This could include regulatory and statutory obligations, meeting client SLAs, meeting outside counsel guidelines, complying with clients' billing requirements, and similar. All of these kinds of factors need to be considered as part of any innovation project, and, crucially, considered early on.

Lawyers, despite the appearance they can on occasion give, don't know everything. They tend to have a deep, narrow specialism – for example, a seasoned civil litigator is unlikely to have a deep knowledge of the GDPR – which the organization will need to take into account when looking at solutions. We have found it is always easiest to address potential data-related issues early and head on. There is nothing worse than everyone proceeding thinking that something is possible when in fact it is contrary to some GDPR or data rule.

Having a solution before you know what the problem is

Capacity management, in the sense of the optimal number of lawyers to work on a given volume of matters, has always interested us. We could even draw what we wanted it to look like so that you had a calendar view of where the peaks and troughs were likely to arise on a set of files so you knew who to give a new file to and whether you needed to recruit to deal with workload. We have never got very far with it – not everyone agreed that utilization was an issue, or at least that knee-jerk recruitment was the cause of the problem.

We have seen many, many start-ups over the years that were started by disenfranchised lawyers. As one senior law firm executive explained in The Law Society's report on lawtech adoption:

> *"I find the start-ups hard to engage with. Some that I have had dealings with seem to be set up by a disgruntled lawyer who happened to go to uni with an IT guy. I just feel that very few of them are actually doing anything new and tend to fall into three main types: they're generating documents, reviewing and analyzing documents, or analyzing Management Information such as legal spend or workflow. They are not necessarily reinventing the wheel but looking to provide a shinier newer wheel."*[5]

It is important when you are looking to solve a problem or are seeing a tech demo that you keep this in mind and do not assume that every lawyer working in the same area has the same problem (and indeed works in the same way – often the start-up lawyers seem to be solving a problem specific to the way they worked, which often is not something of wider applicability).

As we have been writing this book, generative AI has been the discussion point of the moment, not just in law firms but in society in general, with ChatGPT amassing over 100 million users within two months of launch.[6] Specific use cases are beginning to emerge, but there does perhaps need to be some caution. In particular, what is the problem to which the answer is a solution that is unreliable? Our current view is that generic LLMs are likely to have slightly more utility in the hands of a domain expert (who is able to filter out the hallucinations and other nonsense answers) than someone who is trying to acquire new knowledge in any given domain. However, like everyone else, we are still working out the implications of LLMs within our business and our clients' businesses.

Spending time on the urgent rather than the important

With so many things to do in the world of innovation, there can be a tendency to keep working on what is immediately in front of you. There is always a full inbox, a lack of resource, more ideas than you know what to do with, law firm politics, and usually something on fire that needs to be dealt with. All of this can mean that you end up focusing on the urgent things, rather than the more important, often strategic things.

There is no magic wand to fix this, but accepting the reality that you are never going to get everything done can help you deal with it. You might want to block out larger chunks of time in your calendar to do the actual thinking, which can often lead to being able to delegate or set different timeframes for that urgent work. As the saying goes, "Your failure to prepare does not constitute an emergency for me" – worth remembering when the pressure is on. Time not dealing with the day-to-day job of innovation is important in order to get some perspective on what you are trying to achieve and to learn from other areas of industry as to what approaches might work and what might not. Attend conferences, read books on other topics, and listen to experts in other areas – innovative ideas often present themselves when you are not focusing on them.

Failing – not enough?

As part of a business services function, you are always inherently aware of the need to justify your existence and show your worth (regardless of whether this is a message pushed in your organization). This amplifies as you grow the size of a team as your decisions now do not just impact your career, but those around you too. Against this is the fact that we know not everything that we try will be successful, and indeed it should not be, otherwise it is not innovation! The difference in rhetoric versus reaction in terms of showing worth compared to trying things that do not ultimately work is likely to determine ultimately how successful your innovation efforts are. We are lucky in that we have strong Board support for our endeavors, including the element of experimentation that is required. Failure is acceptable, provided that lessons are learned (and the same failure does not reoccur). It goes against our better nature to fail, but we have tried to normalize this as part of the innovation function. We commend failure as evidence that the innovation team is doing their job and look to understand why something did not work or what can be changed. Projects have a lesson-learned session, which is an open discussion of what could be done differently in future, but in order to improve things rather than attribute blame.

Chapter checklist

- ☐ What is the attitude in your organization to failure?
- ☐ Where aspects of previous projects in your organization have failed, do they follow any repeated themes?
- ☐ How are decisions made in your organization – is HIPPO a problem?
- ☐ Are you solving problems rather than symptoms?

References

1 The legal industry is now applying LLMs to this problem and it will be interesting to follow how this experiment pans out over the next few years.

2 Gagnon, J., "IBM Watson Health's Challenges Tell Us More About Healthcare Data Than It Does About AI", Forbes, May 2022. See: www.forbes.com/sites/forbestechcouncil/2022/05/03/ibm-watson-healths-challenges-tell-us-more-about-healthcare-data-than-it-does-about-ai/?sh=77c0d6a25b48.

3 See case study in chapter seven.

4 See chapter three in relation to prioritization of pilots and what to work on.

5 The Law Society, "Lawtech adoption by the legal profession", February 2019. See: www.lawsociety.org.uk/topics/research/lawtech-adoption-report.

6 Hu, K., "ChatGPT sets record for fastest-growing user base - analyst note", Reuters, February 2023. See www.reuters.com/technology/chatgpt-sets-record-fastest-growing-user-base-analyst-note-2023-02-01/.

Chapter 9: **If you build it, who will come?**

Innovation is all about people and process first, or at least we think so. We have talked elsewhere about there not being a magic technology wand that in and of itself is a solution to, well, pretty much anything in a law firm, despite the latest hype around generative AI and LLMs. Even, for example, document review technology does not solve all of the problem all by itself – although we find it often halves the time that people take to undertake document review. It still needs people, and we still need a process – to make sure documents are passed to the software, that the software is trained, that the system then extracts all of the relevant clauses, and for someone to review the extracted clauses.

We feel the hardest part of innovation is adoption beyond the pilot. Adoption in particular relies on people and process; if you do not have a particular process, or even if you do have a process, if people do not follow that process, then adoption is a seriously uphill battle. Without these preconditions, for some of the people your innovation solution simply will not be solving their particular problem and so in fact has no use to them whatsoever. We have seen this with the explosion of legal tech start-ups in the last five or six years where, in our experience, there were a lot of solutions wandering around looking for problems to solve. One of the giveaway red flags is when the start-up talks about software designed by lawyers for lawyers. A good number of these start-ups solved the problem the particular lawyer had because of the way that that particular lawyer worked without, seemingly, much actual testing to see if other lawyers worked in the same way and had the same problem.

Part of the challenge for innovation (especially where it involves technology) is that quite often there is no single right way for a lawyer to achieve a client's outcome; more often than not there are lots of equally legitimate approaches. We have seen people in the same team, doing the same work for the same client, working in entirely different ways – ranging from making use of the workflow technology solution to creating an entirely parallel solution using Excel.

From pilot to roll-out – hurdles, pitfalls, and the problem of reacting to anecdote rather than data

Despite having planned the pilot meticulously and having carefully thought through all the potential issues discussed in chapter three, often the first hurdle you encounter when looking to evaluate the success of the pilot is working out if it is complete. This sounds counter intuitive. Of course, as part of your planning you would have given the pilot an end date, but often things do not run to plan: someone in the team is off ill and everyone else is covering their work with no time for a pilot; the deal you thought you would test the technology on is delayed; urgent new instructions come in that do not align with the technology use case. In chapter three, we recommended check-in calls during the pilot with the external provider, which can also be used to look at usage levels. Generally, your technology providers will a) know their product better than you and b) want their technology to succeed and thus working with them should maximize the chances of the pilot succeeding. The temptation is to continue a pilot until X more documents have been reviewed or users have logged on Y more times, but a decision has to be made as to when enough data is enough to enable you to review the pilot outcomes. This needs to be weighed against extending the pilot period, which can affect other innovation projects or result in a flurry of use in the last couple of days.

When you are satisfied that your pilot has ended, you can then review the feedback and data, and evaluate that against the success criteria. Again, this is not as straightforward as it sounds – often, you will find that a certain group of pilot users find it more useful than another. This could be due to their level of experience, meaning that they find the system more helpful than someone with more expertise. It may be that the theory was better than the practical application and whilst the technology in the pilot has solved a problem, or at least part of one, it has created other issues, not all of which can have been expected (and users do not always use things in the way they are intended!).

With a bit of luck (and careful planning), you will have lots of information to review in order to determine whether your pilot has been a success (either in the way envisaged or an unexpected way) or a failure. There is usually data around usage or time to review. You need to know what your benchmark figures are for doing the same (or as similar as you can get) work or project so you have something to compare with what actually happened in the pilot. Do not necessarily discount a smaller time saving than you were anticipating

– a small time saving repeated every day by a large number of people adds up to a big time saving overall. Also, at this stage, you and your users are going to be at their absolute worst at using the technology – it is unfamiliar, they have not worked out the best way of using it, and (usually) the technology will only get better. It also depends on the problem you are trying to solve. A marginal gain on an individual matter can mount up to a substantial cumulative saving over a collection of matters.

This is where making a sensible extrapolation of the data can help. By sensible, we mean don't say you are going to have 100 percent adoption and for it to be used on 100 percent of all matters as that is unrealistic. Look at previous levels of similar work and the fee earner profile and extrapolate cautiously. Use your legal experts to get a steer on what the market in that area looks like. Is there more of the work you could be doing if you could do it quicker? Are there unmet legal needs that could be met if the technology could meet the needs at a price point the clients are prepared to pay (see the Equality Act 2010 example in chapters five and seven)? Could the technology let you do the work at a different level or change your supervision pattern? All of these factors are useful pieces of information to pull into a series of extrapolations of best, worst, and realistic figures, with a set of assumptions provided for each set of figures. This can then be used to shape a business case, or any other document you might need to secure budget.

There is also usually qualitative data to explore alongside the quantitative data. This may have been collected during focus groups, casual chats, or feedback surveys. Sometimes, the technology providers mandate their method of feedback as part of the pilot. At first we went along with this but now we do not let that happen. Beware the tech provider that tries to meet users on their own to divide and conquer the users or insist partner X wants a technology or, worse still, says partner X has signed a license (and obviously doesn't hold a budget!).

If your pilot has imposed a process, or required people to actually follow an ignored process, then your pilot and any subsequent adoption is going to be like pushing water uphill. Our experience is that if you find yourself in this position then you may not be solving the right problem, and we would question the value of a pilot. Even a good solution will not be easily accepted if people have to change the entire way they have been working. Unlearning one way of working and learning another is always painful and will, for some weeks at least, slow them down – in those circumstances your solution will be associated with, and take the blame for, that pain, whatever the longer-term benefits might be. As we discussed in chapter three, being really clear on the success criteria and garnering a wide range of feedback (including looking for any unintended consequences) is key to running and evaluating a pilot.

When watching demos, it is always worth asking questions about:

- What does the onboarding and roll-out look like – how has it been successful with other firms e.g., phased roll-out?
- What does training and its method of delivery look like – training modules or live sessions?
- How will they keep you up to date with new functionality?
- How, typically, do other customers keep their users up to date with new functionality?
- Do you get a customer success manager?

You need to gauge how much support you will get from the technology provider as this will affect the people you need to allocate to the roll-out and how the lawyers take to the technology.

What are you measuring – what does adoption success look like?
The easiest way of explaining what adoption success looks like is to detail a case study where the stars aligned and we got it more right than wrong.

Case study: Email filing assistant (EFA)

Challenge/opportunity
We manage and document all of our matters using a CMS, regardless of the type of work. This means all incoming and outgoing communications (including emails and post) are saved against the relevant client and matter number in the CMS, providing an auditable, matter-centric view of all of our matters. There is an administrative overhead in saving an incoming email into the right matter. It takes a number of clicks to go through the "save wizard", which takes, on average, 30 seconds a time. Our case handlers, understandably, find this irritating as they have to do it many times through the day. It is even less user-friendly if you were out of the office for any period of time with access to emails only via your mobile, in which case the emails would need to be saved into the relevant matters on return to the office – the last thing you feel like doing after a day spent travelling.

Where outgoing emails are generated from the CMS, it tags the email with the relevant client and matter number and incoming replies to those outgoing emails retain that tag. Conceptually, therefore, it seemed possible to automatically store tagged emails into the right matter in the CMS and remove some friction for case handlers, but this was not functionality provided within the CMS.

As a full-service national firm, the solution had to take into account many different approaches to workflow across the firm to be scalable. Unlike lots of innovation, this was aiming to solve a firm-wide problem, not just one for a single team or use case.

Strategy

The objective of the project was to develop a new method of email filing, automating this process entirely to relieve users of the task of filing emails and their attachments into the CMS document management system, resulting in cost and time savings as well as reducing friction and frustration.

The innovation team began work and instructed some external collaborators (a consultancy firm and a firm specializing in RPA) to work alongside them. The strategy was to automate the process by leveraging RPA and machine learning software so that we could run a proof of concept to see what was technically possible. We would then engage teams on a trial basis before passing the project to the business change team to scale and roll-out to the entire firm. Conceptually, it sounded relatively straightforward but the devil was, inevitably, in the detail. Having dealt with the necessary detail we ran a small, successful, pilot with eight case handlers. Feedback was positive in terms of the time saved for case handlers. Feedback from the pilot also allowed us to iterate, such as adding an Outlook flag that identified whether the incoming email had been filed or not.

People

The whole project was focused on the end user experience. Our experience of legal specific technology over the last 15 years of procuring, implementing, using, maintaining, and upgrading legal technology is that, generally, the development money goes in to features and functionality rather than UX.

We engaged with many people across the firm in getting to the nub of the problem and designing a solution built from user feedback, testing it on a group of eight people from around the business before a wider user pilot. Our approach to the proof of concept was that this was only worth doing if it improved the experience of the people using our system – if we were being trendy we would say we adopted a (legal) design thinking or service design mindset.

Execution

After a successful proof of concept, the filing system was piloted with 50 case handlers over a two-week period. The innovation team used a variety of internal communication methods to reach out to the pilot users and note any observations or concerns. This included email contact, face-to-face meetings, and instant messenger. Progress was monitored regularly and tweaked for improved user experience. The solution saved 4,700 emails in ten days and the pilot feedback was very positive.

Outcome

However, the project was about more than delivering operational efficiency – the innovation team wanted to add value to the internal customer experience, be more agile, and take another step towards creating a more intelligent working environment. The new functionality was impressive:

- There is dedupe functionality so it only saves an email once, even if it is sent to multiple people.
- We added a function to enable case handlers to easily add a meaningful description to the saved email, should they wish to.
- It checks document numbers before saving to ensure multiple documents are not saved.
- It selects the correct associate to save against using metadata within the email.
- Emails are filed when people send them from their mobile device.

Following the successful pilot, EFA was then rolled out across the firm to, at that stage, the remaining 800 case handlers using similar tactics to communicate and support the team managers and individuals. On roll-out, we received a lot of positive comments. One partner commented, unsolicited:

> *"The new saving mail mechanism is really, REALLY helpful ... Seriously – for someone who might leave their desk for two minutes and then come*

back to a sea of new emails, it is utterly brilliant – well done to whoever orchestrated that."

Rightly or wrongly, we added the ability to enable or disable the functionality based on personal choice. Of circa 850 case handlers, we had 802 using the functionality, meaning despite some rejections we have had a 94 percent adoption rate. A testament to solving the right problem, for most people at least. In terms of ROI, saving 30 seconds of time per email saves, across the firm, something in the region of 12,000 hours. If you multiply that by an average recovery rate, it is fair to say that the system pays for itself many times over. So much so, the solution is being implemented via an external partner to other law firms using the CMS and we receive direct revenue from those implementations.

We built it, they came (most of them, at least).

What did we learn?

- *Meddling with core systems is a whole new level of risk compared to a standalone cloud-based pilot.* We had to meddle with two core systems for us – emails and the CMS. They are so business critical that we had to ensure our testing was rigorous before roll-out; even then, working on two core systems at the same time was a necessary risk to solve the problem.
- *Emotions play a bigger role in innovation than you might think.* Our case handlers rationally understand the need to file emails, documents, and letters. This filing is necessary for day-to-day operations and provides future benefits, like the ability to search and filter the Document Management System (DMS). However, on an emotional level, case handlers experience immediate discomfort when filing emails for a future benefit that isn't immediately visible. This task is particularly frustrating because a) they deal with a large number of emails daily; b) filing each email takes a measurable amount of time; and c) emails sometimes come in so quickly that they need to be saved later.
- *You cannot over-involve users.* Experience dictated from earlier proof of concepts in other circumstances that whilst it appears to be a relatively simple problem, getting adoption requires the involvement of end users throughout the process to address the details.
- *External collaborators having skin in the game is important.* All parties shared the risk, including the consultancy firm, the RPA

specialists, and us in that all parties committed time to the proof of concept with no guarantee of success or future engagement, but all parties could see that it should be possible to solve and the rewards had the potential to be very high.

Innovation solutions becoming business-as-usual – how do you gather momentum and let go?

The danger with pilots is that they involve willing people who have given a lot of support to make the pilot a success. However, when you roll-out to a wider group, where you have potentially less engaged people with less support and hand-holding, then the success of the pilot is not always replicated. There are several things you can do to try and prevent against this:

- *Continue to provide support*. Timing is everything and if you have the capacity available within the team, gently phasing out support is by far the most effective way that we have found to encourage longer-term adoption. The support does not need to be at the same level as the pilot, but making it clear that you are available to help can go a long way to alleviate the concerns of the wider group. You want to limit the range of possible excuses for not using the technology.
- *Keep the communications rolling*. Technology adoption is typically slow and steady initially until it gets some momentum, and then it starts picking up everything and everyone in sight! It is important to keep the (positive) communication rolling after a pilot ends. You can share short case studies and examples of use cases, attend relevant team meetings to update on any new features, answer queries or just generally promote the use (it is hard to ignore you if you turn up to a meeting rather than email).
- *Lean on your customer success manager*. Most suppliers now have customer success managers as they have realized that it is harder work to win new clients as opposed to dealing with renewals. They are usually an excellent source of tips and tricks to encourage uptake, or happy to put you in touch with peers in other firms to share how they have encouraged adoption (sometimes name-dropping another firm is the encouragement people need to give the technology a try). Often, customer success managers have been lawyers and so understand the type of work that the teams are trying to use the technology on. This can help generate some imaginative ways to use the technology. They also may have access to more tailored training materials that you can use.

- *Make it competitive or use a recognition platform*. On some pieces of technology, we feed back to the department head on the number of people who have used it each month so that they can help monitor and encourage usage. Sometimes sharing these statistics with the team using it can encourage a bit of friendly rivalry. Saying thanks and well done to people on firm recognition platforms, or getting more senior people to do this, can also nudge people towards increased adoption rates.
- *Create your own training*. Although it can be tempting to use a supplier's training material, as a sweeping generalization they can often be a bit long and are not optimized for the lawyer in a hurry to engage with. We have found creating FAQ documents and short training materials on specific and relevant points have a better uptake than longer supplier materials.
- *Have a mechanism for capturing new starters and trainees*. Making sure you offer training to new starters as they join the team, or trainees as they move around the firm, is important to ensure that you do not get pockets of people who do not know about the technology or how to use it. Again, communication with the relevant department head can help with this as they can advise who needs access and if they have experience with the technology.

Following the crowd – adoption because everyone else is using it

It is rare to find two lawyers who would go about solving the same legal problem in an absolutely identical way, but when it comes to technology, partners (in particular) seem to want to follow the crowd and ensure they are using the same technology as other firms. We have discussed this in chapter eight in relation to when things go wrong.

It felt like we had moved away from PR-driven innovation, but while writing this book, not a day has gone by where generative AI has been out of the headlines or LinkedIn posts. Initially the hype was around the publicly available LLMs but this quickly shifted to models aimed at legal use cases, or from the mainstream technology and law publishers. Generative AI has captured the imaginations of law firm C-suites in a way that the metaverse and blockchain did not. It is arguably too early to know the full extent of the impact of LLMs on the professional service world, but the C-suite is no doubt thinking about productivity, profitability, and what a workforce may look like in an LLM-dominated world. When discussions around a single technology start to dominate in a profession, this can be hard to steer an organization through as there is both excitement around it and anxiety about being left behind. There will always be trends and dealing with them often requires going back to first principles:

- Ask "What is the problem you are trying to solve?" before working out the way to solve it, which may or may not include the technology trend of the moment. Make sure you fully understand the problem and use case before you start going anywhere near solutions.
- Understand what the current processes are, whether they remain fit for purpose, and what changes may be required as part of figuring out the solution, including how any new technology would work.
- For the particular problem, use case, or new technology, where do you want to be on the curve – innovators or with the early majority? This is likely to vary depending on your strategic focus and (if there is already an existing solution in place) how much of an enhancement the new technology trend may represent. The longevity of a solution, the level of risk your firm tolerates, whether you want to go with emerging or more established technology, the cost, the interoperability, whether the technology is internal- or external-facing are all factors that will affect this discussion.

Chapter checklist

- ☐ How do you know when a pilot is finished?
- ☐ Have you got a plan for taking successful pilots into wider adoption?
- ☐ What does successful technology adoption look like?
- ☐ How can you encourage long-term technology adoption?

Chapter 10: Barriers

Barriers to implementing innovation can come in several guises and, as you may anticipate, some of them are easier to overcome than others. In true lawyer style, this book is not intended as legal advice so in this chapter we consider in broad terms some of the regulatory, people, and organizational issues you may face, without dwelling on the specific legal requirements to overcome them, not least as the landscape for innovation regulation is evolving.

Professional obligations

Solicitors and law firms are subject to many professional obligations, in part to uphold the constitutional principle of the rule of law, but also importantly to uphold public trust in the legal profession. In England and Wales, the Solicitors Regulation Authority (SRA) is the body that regulates solicitors on, importantly, both an individual and organizational level, and the law firm organizations in which they work. Other jurisdictions will have similar oversight bodies, such as the ABA in America. The SRA has a set of guiding principles and a Code of Conduct (the Code), which in 2011 changed from having a rules-based approach to being outcome-focused regulation. The way law firms service their clients is included within this, so when using AI or other innovation, law firms need to act in accordance with the guidance so that trust is maintained, equality and diversity is encouraged, and the best interests of each client are acted on within solicitors' overarching obligations to uphold the rule of law. Keeping the affairs of clients confidential unless disclosure is required or permitted by law, or the client consents, is a key outcome under the Code, in addition to the common law right of confidentiality (amongst other tortious, fiduciary, and contractual obligations). In an innovation context, this means thinking upfront about maintaining client confidentiality as you explore and pilot new technology or develop new ways of servicing clients – what data you can use and how you minimize access to it are key considerations.

This issue has come to the forefront in relation to LLMs and generative AI, where you can provide the model with documents that ground your context, in theory resulting in a more accurate outcome, but meaning you need to allow the model to look at your data. LLMs are data-hungry, and any exchange of data and steps taken to mitigate data risks with providers needs to be carefully documented – including what data is being accessed, where the data is processed, how the data is processed, and what, if any, data is stored and where.

The SRA guidance, being outcome-focused, has a degree of flexibility in an attempt to keep pace with an everchanging landscape. In relation to innovation, in April 2024, the Legal Standards Board[1] published Statutory Guidance on promoting technology and innovation to improve access to legal services.[2] This work began in 2021 when it identified the topic as important to help address the challenge of legal services that better meets society's needs. Whilst this was being drafted, LLMs exploded onto the technological scene and it is unclear the extent to which they were considered in the process. The stance of the guidance is technology-neutral and pro-innovation and we expect regulators such as the SRA to continue in the same vein.

Of course, maintaining levels of trust in part means giving correct advice, and this is no different if technology is used to assist a lawyer or not. In some respects, the use of AI is no different from using a reputable case law tool; at the end of the day the lawyer remains responsible for the accuracy. The technology is another set of tools for a lawyer to use to augment their expertise, rather than replace it. The user should have training on the technology so they can operate it efficiently and, crucially, understand the good and bad use cases for it. Technology should be tested so that firms are satisfied that the outcomes are at least as good as, if not better than, the more traditional comparable service to the client. Sandbox environments, which are an isolated testing environment, are a good way to explore a new piece of technology as an innovation team and with end users, before bringing it into your infrastructure.

It remains unknown as to whether we are likely to see liability attached for a failure to use AI technology. The Master of the Rolls, Sir Geoffrey Vos KC, suggested that this day would come "soon",[3] which is suitably vague in terms of timescales, but will no doubt become more of a consideration for lawyers. If you have access to a document review system with a level of accuracy that is at least as good as the more traditional manual way, does this need to be offered to a client? It can be hard to work out the cost impact on the client as, although you may now be able to do the work quicker, you have had the technology, training, and piloting overhead to consume as part of your business. Our case study in chapter six explores how we dealt with the option of manual or technology-assisted document review for a client.

Have regulatory obligations kept step with technological advancements?
Given the speed at which the technology landscape evolves, outcomes-based regulation is perhaps the only way to provide a framework for those undertaking innovation in professional firms to advance it, without having to wait for prescriptive legislation to keep up. As we all know, regulation can never keep up with technological advances. The (acceptable) use of AI in general has become a topic for societal and political discussion and we now have an Office for Artificial Intelligence, which published a policy paper in March 2023 expounding a pro-innovation approach to AI regulation.[4] Hot on its heels in November 2023, the UK hosted an AI Safety Summit with representatives from 29 countries in attendance, including key leaders on the global stage. The outcome of this event is what is known as The Bletchley Declaration[5] – an international affirmation that to be good for all and to ensure AI can achieve its transformative positive potential, *"AI should be designed, developed, deployed, and used, in a manner that is safe, in such a way as to be human-centric, trustworthy and responsible"*.[6] A focus on human centricity echoes our innovation approach, which considers technology as augmentation to the expertise of our lawyers.

Do you know what is in your contracts with your clients and suppliers?
We know that lawyers love small print, and it is particularly important that contractual small print is reviewed in an innovation context. As we will explain in chapter 11, working closely with your risk and compliance teams can prevent an unwelcome surprise late in the day. In relation to knowing what is in your contracts, this takes a couple of different angles depending on which capacity you are acting in, but things to consider aside from the usual termination and usage clauses include:

- *Using technology – your firm's terms and conditions:*
    - Can you use anonymized data for innovation – are there limits on the type of data?
    - Does your client care letter have an innovation paragraph?
    - Do you specifically refer to pieces of technology, or is that simply how you perform your legal services?
    - Are technology costs passed on as a disbursement and, if the tech-

nology is a platform with, for example, a yearly storage charge, is that made clear?

- *Using technology – clients' terms and conditions:*
  - Is there a specific innovation clause?
  - What limits does your client put on what you can do with their data?
  - If you are using specific technology, does this require client permission and is this on a case-by-case basis or a one-off authorization?
  - Do you have to provide data back in a prescribed format?
- *Procuring technology to use – suppliers' terms and conditions:*[7]
  - What are the limits on what the supplier can do with data you supply?
  - Where do backups go, how are they stored and retained?
  - Is the technology built on other proprietary technology and, if so, are there things you need to be aware of in relation to the main contract (this has been an issue in relation to LLMs and retention of materials for abuse monitoring by the main supplier for 28 days when it was used in other technology)?

Data concerns – GDPR

On 2 May 2018, the EU General Data Protection Regulation (GDPR) replaced the UK's Data Protection Act 1998. Following Brexit, this has now been enshrined in our domestic legislation as the snappily titled UK GDPR. Discussions prior to the implementation of GDPR made it seem a bit like the millennium bug, whereby everything would come to a halt as it came into force. In reality, law firms have always been extremely careful with data – one would argue that their professional obligations to keep the affairs of clients confidential is far wider than their obligations under GDPR. The UK GDPR applies to data controllers and processers where the processing is carried out by organizations that operate within the UK and, in an innovation context, this is highly likely to apply to your projects. Article 22 of the UK GDPR requires, with very limited exceptions, individuals to give explicit consent in scenarios where solely automated decision-making is being carried out that has a legal, "or similarly significant" impact on them. This means that in the vast majority of scenarios, a computer alone, without consent, cannot decide on a legal problem without some human oversight and involvement. Completing Data Protection Impact Assessments to document the steps you are taking to minimize data protection risks in conjunction with your risk team can help to ensure that you are taking a proportionate approach to data issues.

Perhaps because both of us are lawyers, we have always been keen to ensure that our innovation projects that use AI do so in an explainable and transparent manner, not least because we know to get lawyers to trust and use AI they would need to have, at least at some level, an understanding of how it works.

People and organizational barriers

Throughout this book, we have stressed that innovation in law firms is a people game. In all reality, people are likely to be your biggest barrier. The actual structure of a law firm, usually a partnership model with decisions taken by a Board often full of partners, or alternatively a structure where an individual equity partner[8] can veto a particular decision or project, can also make it cumbersome to attempt to be innovative.

Chargeable hours – a help or a hinderance?

Life in a law firm revolves around six-minute increments of time, day in and day out, as lawyers bill in these six-minute units. Even when on a fixed fee arrangement, the act of recording time enables a firm to understand how long they are taking on a particular matter (which will more than likely change with the degree of seniority of the lawyer) and, in turn, whether the work can be performed profitably. This preoccupation with the importance of time means that lawyers split their time into periods of chargeable (legal work that will be billed) and non-chargeable (everything else that is not billable, such as admin, billing, or training). You can see the issue already. In our view, innovation requires multi-disciplinary teams to work at solving problems together, rather than just a business services team who may not fully understand the client issue or context, let alone the legal analysis. Innovation projects, as we have discussed in earlier chapters, work best when you have an involved, interested, and knowledgeable lawyer acting as a subject matter expert. These people will also have chargeable hours and revenue targets and innovation projects often fall into the non-chargeable time category. This means that, even with the best of intentions, chargeable hours will remain the focus for all but the most eager of subject matter experts, unless you can do something to change the dynamic. Some firms have made temporary secondments into innovation teams; others have allowed time for non-chargeable innovation to "count" for the purpose of showing a commitment to case handlers' hours or financial targets, perhaps offering 50 hours per year towards an innovation project.

We knew that we would not get very far attempting to enact innovation if it was just us and a handful of legal engineers as we would need input from subject matter experts to solve problems for clients. We could only get so far leveraging our experience with clients when we last practiced (thankfully not a lot had changed in the meantime) and knew we would have to enlist the support of a broader cohort to accelerate our work. This meant attempting to do something creative to free up time for people who could help, so that they had the opportunity to work on projects with us. We considered an innovation chargeable time dispensation, which was rejected – with hindsight, we probably asked for this too early for us to have something we could use to show it was worth the investment. We are also not convinced that, in practice, it would have worked and accelerated our projects. A total of 50 hours might sound like a lot, but when you need to involve people who are not used to working on projects, let alone innovation ones, you can rapidly burn through that time. Many people with 50 hours of time find that hard to manage and, by the time that they are getting useful, their hours will be completed. If you have to keep rotating lawyers onto projects (getting them up to speed each time), it can be hard to show a Board ROI on the investment of this time, which would otherwise have been spent on hours billed to a client.

Working on Peter Drucker's principle of "what gets measured gets done", as we stepped into new roles as the product and innovation department was formed, we created the role of product and innovation partner and we "measured" what they did. As detailed in chapter four, these are partners whose focus for the majority of their time (60 percent) is on product and innovation. This means every three weeks, we are getting the equivalent of a subject matter expert with a 50-hour annual innovation target. Assuming a 48-week working year, each product and innovation partner is the equivalent of having 16 lawyers freed up for 50 hours, with the added benefit that they are constantly being upskilled and using that additional knowledge on subsequent projects, which you do not get if you keep rotating in new lawyers.

Trainees and apprentices are also a useful group to work with, because they tend to have reduced chargeable hours pressure and time to learn new things as part of their training. They are used to having to learn new things in a relatively short six-month period of time before moving around a law firm. The fact that they move around your business also means that they can act as champions and sources of referral back into the innovation team. You will have taught them how to break down a problem and work with people to understand how to solve it, and this insider steer from a trainee in a team who is actually doing the work is invaluable. We started offering trainees the chance to spend six months with us very early on and have now had over 12 trainees and apprentices complete six months with us, and then return to other teams. They tend to keep in touch, are a rich source of ideas, and are a great group for us to test ideas out on.

Does the partnership model inhibit innovation?

Law firms remain pyramid-shaped in hierarchy, and there is no doubt that the closer to the top of the pyramid you can get those leading your innovation efforts, the easier time they will have advancing the innovation agenda. This is relatively speaking, as all innovation in law firms is still difficult. Innovation in law firms is increasingly recognized as a career path and, for one of your authors and in other firms, this has been the route to partnership promotion when firms are keen to signal internally and externally that innovation is an important part of the firm's approach to working with their clients.

Of course, structure in and of itself solves nothing. You always end up with a similar set of constraints in organizations; too much to do and not enough people, time, money, or a combination of the three to do it. What does matter is the decision-making structure in your organization so that you can be nimble in your innovation efforts. This depends on the nature of your Board and what decisions it can make. If, like ours, it is enabled to make decisions with delegated authority then this means you can influence them to get things done. If your structure means that one equity partner can veto any decision, then it is going to be much harder to get things done. In the innovation arena, you are highly unlikely to be pleasing all of your equity partners at the same time, especially given lawyers' tendencies to prioritize their own client's problems.

Without a Board-level mandate, it is hard, if not impossible, to attempt innovation. However, this mandate must be put into action to be effective. This means that the behaviors required for successful innovation are rewarded, blockers (such as lack of time) are removed, and fast failure is accepted. This then gives you a remit to push innovation and deal with resistance at an organizational level. To test our Board's appetite for innovation, several years ago we asked for money, internal people (and people to backfill the roles that those people vacated), and a healthy training budget. This was all agreed and we have made and received subsequent additional rounds of investment. In general, such a vote of confidence from the Board does wonders to get partners on side.

The psychology of lawyers

There are many studies on the personality traits of lawyers, with Dr Larry Richard at the forefront of this topic for many years.[9] Accepting this is a sweeping generalization, Dr Richard's work[10] shows that lawyers tend to score, compared to the "general" population:

- Highly for skepticism – "judgmental, questioning, argumentative and somewhat self-protective";
- Highly for urgency – "characterized by impatience, a need to get things done, a sense of immediacy";
- Low for sociability – meaning they "are more likely to rely on relationships that already exist";
- Low for resilience – "people who are low on resilience tend to be defensive, resist taking in feedback and can be hypersensitive to criticism"; and
- Highly for "herding cats – autonomy" – "it's common for lawyers to resist being managed, to bridle at being told what to do, and to prize their independence".

When you see this written down, it is no wonder that innovation in law firms is hard! You are asking a bunch of highly skeptical people who like to have things done immediately, to meet people they may not know to discuss different ways of solving a problem and in a project that they will not own. To be clear, all these traits are the sorts of things you want to see from a highly successful lawyer (and as Dr Richard argues is to be expected), but that does not detract from the point that all of the things that one might regard as strengths for a lawyer advising clients may not necessarily be a strength from the point of view of an organization that wants to innovate and effect change.

Understanding your clients – how to help those who do not know what they want

As we noted in chapter two, the impetus for law firms to undertake innovation came from a client driver to "be more innovative" and "deliver innovation". The trouble with this is that no one knew what it meant, including the clients who were asking for it. Usually, they were facing internal pressure to deliver more for less, or quicker, and were then pushing this to their suppliers, including their law firms. Of course, this can be resolved by asking clients what they mean, but here is the first challenge. As in most organizations, there are gate-keepers to clients. They are often very senior, experienced partners who may have been involved with the particular client for a very long time. They may have nurtured this relationship for many years and know them inside out. They may not be very keen on technology and would not consider themselves best placed to have a chat to the client about what the client means by innovation. Hearing firsthand from a client, with the opportunity to ask questions and go wherever the conversation may lead is very powerful and hugely helpful in your innovation role. However, given the personality traits described above, they may also not be that predisposed to someone new speaking to a client to ask them questions that no one knows the answer to – all their worst nightmares potentially rolled into one.

It can require some delicate political maneuvering to even get to the place where your gate-keeper is happy for you to have the conversation. Fear of missing out is a powerful motivator, and you only really need one or two to let you over the threshold to have those conversations before the rest stampede, not wanting their client to miss out on any advantage. This has perhaps been a little easier for us as we were both involved with clients when we practiced so are less of an unknown quantity to introduce to a client. Of course, we bring our junior innovation colleagues to let them prove themselves to the gate-keeper who, in turn, invites them to more client meetings and they, in turn, bring a junior colleague with them – and so the cycle continues.

Even when you get to speak to clients, they do not always know what they want. In the same way that innovation in a law firm is a hearts and mind journey, the same can be said of clients. They will all have different drivers and challenges, different levels of technological understanding, and different levels of acceptance towards change. As inspiration and engagement, you can showcase some of the things you are working on, especially for others in similar businesses, but you need to be prepared to play the long game, keeping communication open, and checking in about current challenges, appetite to risk, and what is keeping them awake at night. A lot of this comes down to timing and sometimes the stars just align. We have one client who we have had innovation exchanges with twice a year for the last three years and, whilst they have been aware of the problem they have been trying to solve, they have not had the appetite or bandwidth to look at solving it. In this particular example, a change of personnel allowed us to explore the problem afresh because it is had moved high enough up their priorities.

You are not Apple

In our managing partner's recent firm update, while discussing innovation, he noted that years ago, we decided we were not going to emulate Apple by selling technology. However, things have changed. Today, we have clients subscribing to software that we have developed in-house using low-code platforms. Interestingly, we don't seem to recall this "ban" and have been building and selling software all along!

It does raise some interesting considerations for those involved in innovation to explore as you look to develop a strategy that will fit in your organization:

- Does your organization have a buy or build preference for technology?
- Do you have the expertise you need within your innovation team or are you going to be dependent on other teams, such as IT, to deliver?
- If you are dependent on other teams, what is your level of dependency, and do they have a well-established system for prioritization?
- If you supply your software to clients:
  - Do clients know how to access you when they are locked out of an account?
  - Do you have service desk hours to deal with queries?
  - Do you triage queries and provide standardized answers as much as possible?
  - How do you obtain client feedback on the software?
  - How do you deal with account management?
  - How do you communicate the software roadmap to them?
  - Crucially, how do you price it?

As law firms become more familiar with the types of innovation that are possible, and more comfortable with it, we will no doubt see a move to productize and commercialize these offerings. We have certainly seen a huge shift in the volume of people who are not surprised when we say a product is a paid-for subscription service, but we can look at what level of subscription is right for a particular client. Even a couple of years ago, this would always be expected to be a value add.

There is always more to do than time and resources allow – how to accept this

An innovation team is usually a cost center for a law firm (although this can change when you start to monetize products), filled with people who are chronically helpful, enjoy problem solving, and like to say yes. This desire to balance your cost, coupled with the knowledge that not all projects will be successful, typically means you say yes to everything and quickly end up with too much on your plate. Usually, the only thing that mitigates this is the fact that the lawyers who said they would come back by a certain date invariably do not, as the demands of their clients naturally take precedence. This gives just enough bandwidth to keep operating, even if it does all feel a bit on the edge – a place where you will have to become comfortable. Much like writing a book, innovation projects tend to take a little bit longer than anticipated, often for perfectly valid reasons.

As you gain experience, you realize that there is a never-ending list of things to do and a limited amount of time and budget, so "no" (or at least, "yes, but") has to be part of your vocabulary. This may mean some projects do not get started, are delivered at a slower pace, or in a different way. As with so much of innovation, clear communication and expectation-setting are key.

We created our own scoring matrix in order to group ideas together to decide on prioritization. It does not really matter what factors you take into account (which will be tailored to your business) or the scoring system that you devise – it is more to have a way of scoring that is applied consistently uniformly as the ideas need to be looked at in the context of an overall firm innovation portfolio. Crucially, it is also presented monthly to our key internal stakeholders including our Board, segment heads, and legal ops directors. We present it with a couple of slides showing the various broad idea groups and with this guidance note blazoned across the front page:

> *"We have divided the ideas into three priority groups, with one being the highest priority. There are a couple of ideas that are unranked for now, but we anticipate would fit into one of the priority categories, e.g. scale/problem currently not scoped, there is some client interest, a chance to do a quick proof of concept, limited by resources. Existing "live" products will also continue. They are detailed on this slide.*
>
> *"The priority category that an idea is in determines the order that they will be worked on, i.e. we would look to progress everything in group one first*

and if there were no outstanding tasks on group one ideas, would move to work on group two etc.
"Some of the ideas are at a very early stage too. The categories do not mean that the product will definitely be made; there may be something that occurs along the way that means the idea is de-prioritized, or no longer works, etc. The converse is also true and things may move up priority groups or indeed move into the groups from the "on hold" list. Lawyer caveats completed, the list is dynamic so please continue to keep ideas coming and let us know of any changes that may mean a previous idea is more relevant. For the avoidance of doubt, within each grouping the ideas are listed alphabetically!"

Prioritizing becomes even harder when you have software being used by clients and you are balancing new ideas against enhancing existing ones. We take new ideas through a vision and discovery session, discussed in chapter three, to explore what the idea is, what the market might be, how we can test client fit, and how we might commercialize it. Some ideas will then follow our "product lite" approach where the idea-proposer is supported through a process that is a longer exploration of the idea, with product and innovation governance and support to help them demonstrate client need and market fit, or to test out an MVP. This means if need and market are established, the idea is already set up in a way that we can easily proceed. We have found this approach works well on ideas where the prioritization may be borderline, but where we think with a bit more work and exploration there is potential.

Chapter checklist

- ☐ Do you know enough about how your regulatory obligations are dealt with in your organization?
- ☐ What are your procurement and supplier management policies – do they need to evolve to promote innovation?
- ☐ Does your organizational structure facilitate innovation?
- ☐ How does your organization prioritize projects and resources?

References

1 The oversight regulator for legal services in England and Wales.
2 "Statutory guidance on promoting technology and innovation to improve access to legal services – response to consultation", April 2024. See: https://legalservicesboard.org.uk/wp-content/uploads/2024/04/Statutory-guidance-on-promoting-technology-%E2%80%93-response-to-consultation.pdf; "Delivering a pro-innovation approach to AI regulation – an outline of the LSB's approach", April 2024. See: https://legalservicesboard.org.uk/news/lsb-publishes-update-on-approach-to-regulating-ai-use
3 Legal Futures. "It will soon be negligent not to use AI, Master of the Rolls predicts", 5 March 2024. See: www.legalfutures.co.uk/latest-news/it-will-soon-be-negligent-not-to-use-ai-master-of-the-rolls-predicts.
4 "A pro-innovation approach to AI regulation", updated August 2023. See: www.gov.uk/government/publications/ai-regulation-a-pro-innovation-approach/white-paper.
5 "The Bletchley Declaration by Countries Attending the AI Safety Summit, 1-2 November 2023". November 2023. See: www.gov.uk/government/publications/ai-safety-summit-2023-the-bletchley-declaration/the-bletchley-declaration-by-countries-attending-the-ai-safety-summit-1-2-november-2023.
6 *Ibid.*
7 Litig has released a questionnaire to use with potential suppliers when producing generative AI. "Litig releases Legal IT AI Due Diligence Questionnaire", May 2024. See: www.litig.org/news/l4zy6wkxepan9gvajgfgeotlsw5opn.
8 Equity partners make an investment into the firm and take a share of the profits.
9 Dr Larry Richard's website, LawyerBrain, contains many of his seminal pieces of research, including: Richard, L., *Herding Cats: The Lawyer Personality Revealed*, August 2002; Richard, L., The Lawyer Types, July 1993; and Richard, L. and Rohrer, L., *A Breed Apart: How personality characteristics (Hogan) influence who becomes a lawyer – and how far they rise*, August 2011. See: www.lawyerbrain.com/downloads/.
10 *Herding Cats: The Lawyer Personality Revealed.*

Chapter 11:
Politics

Those undertaking innovation often find themselves caught in the crossfire between various competing and conflicting demands. Innovation is a team sport, requiring input from different people, many of whom are unlikely to work directly for you and all have their own objectives and competing demands. More than anything else a law firm does, innovation requires you to marshal teams and resources to get to an end solution that ultimately is something you can market and sell, often against a short deadline. You almost always need to think about involving your risk and compliance, IT, and marketing teams, as well as the subject matter expert and their bosses. This chapter explores some of the possible sources of conflict and issues that may arise when navigating internal politics. As it is important to give early notice to internal teams of something coming down the line that requires their involvement, a product lifecycle board can show visually the stages that new ideas are at. We update and circulate this at the start of each month so that internal teams can ask questions about new ideas they may be interested in joining in with, or knowing when they may have to contribute, for example with a request for SSO assistance, help with collateral, or a review of terms and conditions.

Marketing teams – awards and the warm PR glow

Marketing departments often end up with the short straw in law firms – if you lose a tender it is their fault, if you win, it is all down to the partner. The general rule is to be their friend and engage them as fellow professionals. Most humans like to be helpful and like people to appreciate their experience. Seek their help and advice early on, not two days before you want to do a product launch. Just like you, they have a finite amount of resource and time so it is crucial to let them know what might be coming their way.

As you start your first innovation project, you may wonder if you need to involve your marketing team that early, or wait until your project is successful and you have something that can ultimately be sold. Even at the very early stages of your innovation efforts, it is worthwhile getting your marketing team on side. This may involve a monthly catch-up with a campaigns or PR manager, or periodically dropping into team meetings to update them on projects and the type of clients that may be interested. Ideally, you want to sell the innovation dream to your marketing department and have them as active champions, helping you reach external clients and internal client relationship holders. You also do not want to be 90 percent of the way through building your product, only to discover that you have fallen foul of some brand guideline that needs a lot more time and effort to fix. As ever, involving others with differing life experiences can also help generate ideas and approaches that you may not have thought about.

These early conversations with marketing should be two-way; there are lots of things about the working of your marketing department that you will need to know (even if the information is not immediately useful) and this early effort will pay dividends later! It is useful to learn the following about the marketing team:

- Who does what.
- How they approach particular types of clients.
- Who can help with awards nominations.
- What collateral can be produced and how long it takes.
- Their processes.
- What budget they have.
- Where they sit in the change curve.
- Their appetite for innovation.

Innovation may be perceived as a threat, coming in to take resource or get involved in things such as the creation of collateral that historically they have solely been in charge of. Recognizing this as you start engaging with marketing means that you have the opportunity to develop your emotional intelligence and stakeholder management skills (again!). They will often have budgets you do not in your early days, and crucially, they are the best kind of budget as they are not ring-fenced for specific things. This means they can help in ways such as sponsoring events, or with the cost of a table at an awards event. Indeed, their insight can help you decide which awards to enter and how to tailor your award nominations. They also have their own supplier network to whom you can be referred.

When you start with innovation, marketing can often do things that you cannot. They can build campaigns around your product, or if suitable, fit your products into one or more of their existing campaigns. Early in the innovation lifecycle, they can help with market testing, research, and horizon scanning. They can also provide insights about the other areas your organization works in so that you can start to piece together bits of seemingly disparate information. This is when it starts to get exciting, as you can see the opportunity to talk about an idea or product with a different group within your organization and external clients. Occasionally, you have a eureka moment, as these conversations uncover that a product that had a particular use case for one group of clients can be pivoted and adapted to suit another group of clients – this is when you know you have found your scalable and repeatable product. When you are looking at client fit and marketing, they can help work out the best prospects based on their knowledge of your firm's client base and give you guidance on how best to approach those prospects and the internal stakeholder (i.e., the client's relationship partner) based on their knowledge of working with that individual.

Marketing teams approach things from a different perspective and, in particular, can add value and ideas around how to sell the product. Although there may not be the resource to support everything as innovation scales, it is worth taking advantage of all available input when you can early on. A strong early foundation with marketing will help in future projects as there will often be opportunities to recycle successful approaches. Indeed, the more scalable and repeatable you can make all internal processes, the better, as this is likely to be the most efficient delivery method for multiple teams. For us, what started out as a relatively haphazard way of engaging with marketing has developed into a system where:

- There is a shared Teams channel, which houses key documents such as vision documents, roadmaps, the prioritization matrix, and marketing collateral. This is all about making information easy to find and to aid consistency of messaging to the wider organization.
- Innovation processes specifically include marketing involvement early on, using a defined go-to-market process that we developed in conjunction with them.
- There is a monthly product sales meeting that marketing are invited to attend. Teams are encouraged to meet outside of these more formal meetings too.

If you move into productizing your innovation, the marketing team can help with your CRM processes. It is worth taking the time to understand these and marketing's processes, and crucially how they may be adapted to suit information you may need. Our CRM system colleagues are only too happy to talk through the system and build additional modules that collect data to help us understand things like buying lifecycle and how long different products may take to close in different segments. All of which is useful to help you project future revenue with some actual data behind it. It is best to be diligent about working with them – show them that you understand the value of data, of the CRM system and how to use it, and work with them to build innovation into their processes. You are also likely to have to interact with your marketing team to support tenders, and, in the same way you should alert your marketing team of a forthcoming product, you will be grateful for the same courtesy in relation to tenders. The earlier in the tender planning and pipelining process you can be involved, the better – a call late before the deadline is the thing of nightmares. It is useful to have generic copy that can form the first draft of pitch responses, especially in relation to live products and projects, which you can then tailor for the specific client. It is vital that you engage with the marketing team when contributing to pitch responses – ask them what the angle is for the particular pitch and what the client's drivers are to help them make the generic response into a specific one.

IT teams – products, architecture, and security

IT teams have all the tips, tricks, and shortcuts that have been hard won through years of experience with stakeholder management and navigating internal processes to bring in new technology. You are foolish if you do not try and glean some of their best tips as you attempt to tread a similar path in relation to innovation, and ongoing conversations with IT teams are always useful. As always, it is about taking the best bits from what others do and adapting them to fit your processes and context. IT teams have strong project management skills. It was from discussions with the IT team that we got to understand DevOps, which developer teams have used for years. We knew it had some of the functionality we would need to be able to follow the progress of projects and assign tasks and, after some training from our helpful IT colleagues, we set about configuring it for our use case.

Although not every innovation is technology-driven, our experience is that whatever you are doing usually involves some degree of interaction with another system or process. This means that you will be in a queue like the rest of the business. IT departments only have a finite amount of resource and spend a lot of time keeping the lights on and helping users competently navigate the various systems available to them. Setting up your infrastructure to deliver a new product is likely to rank lower than an important security upgrade, for example. Your business will ultimately decide the priorities for the IT department, so working with IT involves a lot of stakeholder management. That said, there are things you can do to influence your position in the queue:

- *Be easy to work with.* Be the ones they want to work with as you cause no hassle, ask for their input, are grateful, and show appreciation. Make their lives easier by finding out what they need from your potential supplier to enable them to check their information security and cybersecurity position, then get this information or materials from the suppliers – it does not take you much time and saves them a job.
- *Let them know what is coming.* Most IT teams will have a long list of things that need to be done, some "background" IT work such as upgrades and patches (the really important operational work which, if it is going well, no one sees), and then work that is driven by business. If you give them early notice of the sorts of things that are coming your way, this enables them to plan in time to work on those things too.
- *Share the information they will need to prioritize you.* If there is a business need for a particular piece of technology then explain what this is, what the impact will be, and if you are able to productize it, what the figures might look like. If there are several options, present them in a useful way, maybe ranking them or explaining why one is preferred to another. If there are peers at other firms who have actual experience of the technology, ask them for things to watch out for. This is all useful intel that can help IT teams evaluate the size of your job.
- *Do not fall into the trap that cloud technology means no IT.* In the same way that innovation teams do not like picking up part-started projects and would prefer to be in from the beginning, IT teams also like early involvement. Even if you are looking at cloud-based software, you are still likely to need some IT help, maybe to set up single sign-on, or at the very least to help you with business continuity solutions for your chosen product.

Case study: Decision support – calculating credit hire

Challenge/opportunity

We handle many motor claims involving credit hire, which has been a perennial problem in the insurance market for over 30 years. Insurer clients are concerned with the general level of expenditure on credit hire and constantly need to consider their handler training to ensure a consistency of approach. Insurers want to ensure that claimants are fairly compensated for losses to which they are legally entitled, but not over-compensated, as this would affect premiums. When dealing with credit-hire claims, handlers need to consider a raft of legal precedent, comparative rates for different vehicles, and perform multiple calculations in order to quantify an offer that reflects the appropriate compensation. This work is time-consuming, laborious, manual, and open to handler subjectivity.

Strategy

We built a solution that uses responses provided by the user to questions that:

- Determines whether a credit-hire claim is valid;
- Calculates the period for which rates should apply, including any variables (e.g., if an intervention offer has been made and more than one rate is applicable for the period of hire);
- Calculates the value of the credit hire claim; and
- Produces a report summarizing and explaining the outcome that is emailed to the handler, creating a clear audit trail.

The innovation team worked in conjunction with our expert lawyers and end users to deliver this project, building the tool to complement a handler's skill set rather than replace them. The tool also addresses other concerns our clients identified around handler training and consistency of approach by guiding users through different pathways based on the information they provide and offering "tool tips" that provide guidance and training.

People

So far, this all sounds plain sailing, but it was actually our second attempt at the credit-hire tool after our first one went wrong. With the best of intentions, everyone was keen to get stuck in on this project and, at the time, try something new. This was one of our earliest attempts at an IT and innovation collaboration where our tool started out being built by our IT developers. We did not fail first time round for lack of willingness from anyone – we failed because we ignored the niggling feeling that this was not the best way to create the tool, but we did not have the skills to build it ourselves and we did not want to offend our colleagues.

The IT team version of the tool reached pilot stage but when we needed to make changes following feedback and to expand the contents of the tool, we slipped slowly down the IT queue as more important projects needed picking up. We lost control in terms of how long it would take to change the tool and send it out to users. We did not waste our time though, we went back to the drawing board to see if we could build the tool in a different way. As a result, the innovation team rapidly upskilled themselves and (successfully) delivered version two of the tool.

Execution

The innovation team worked with our expert lawyers to unpack the decision-making regarding credit hire. The tool contains 91 formulas with 13 different outcomes – significantly reducing the risk of incorrect manual calculations at any stage of the process. The tool was launched internally in August 2021 and tested for a couple of months to successfully validate it before being launched externally.

We analyzed the data of historical cases and those using the tool to be able to calculate the hire saving per file. This calculated field can be:

- Nil, meaning no saving was made;
- A positive figure, meaning that a saving has been made; or
- A negative figure, indicating that the paid figure was higher than the claimed amount.

The data shows that there has been a 3.4 percent saving on small claims files and a 1.86 percent saving on fast-track claims when using the tool. Based on the historical data for one year alone, the financial opportunity gap (had the tool been used on those files) is £90,480, representing a significant opportunity to reduce our clients' indemnity spend by enhancing decision-making consistency.

Outcome

Implementation has been very successful, with the internal use by our lawyers validating the tool. We are firmly of the view that there is no point building tools if users do not trust them so are always keen to collect qualitative data. Since August 2021, we scheduled fortnightly questionnaires for a couple of months so that the users could provide feedback on their experience. A Likert seven scale was used to capture as much granular feedback as possible. The scores indicate that paralegals and trainees were highly favorable about the tool across the board:

- How much easier was it to make decisions using the tool? 5.1/7
- How confident were you using the tool for making decisions on liability/quantum? 5.5/7
- How much did you understand/agree with the decision that the tool reached? 5.8/7
- How much did you trust the tool? 5.5/7
- On a scale of one to ten, how likely are you to recommend the credit hire tool? 8/10

What did we learn?

- *Sometimes you have to take a couple of steps backwards to go forward.* Although building version two of the tool from scratch was initially a backwards step, in this scenario it was absolutely the right thing to do. It allowed us to increase our skill set and to think about the end user perspective and experience in a bit more depth. This has affected our strategy over the years – it was frustrating to need changes to a system that were a priority for us and our internal users, but (understandably) not for our IT teams. We wanted to have software tools that our clients would pay for and use and whilst this may boost our position in the queue, the ability to control the timetable and to surprise and delight our clients wasn't within our control and we realised this wasn't a position we wanted to be in. The development of subsequent tools therefore started from a different place and took into account a much broader set of considerations around deployment and updating the tools than would have been the case without this experience.
- *Do not ignore instincts.* As we have noted elsewhere, the early days of innovation can feel quite insecure. This is especially so if it means declining an offer of help, which in your mind may mean such an

offer may not be forthcoming again (and potentially even offend the rejected party). You will always have internal collaboration and politics in the back of your mind and, early in our innovation work, we lacked the skills to be able to challenge empathetically and listen to our gut feelings (not as the only factor in decision making, but certainly in our experience not one to overlook). Some empathic assertiveness training later, and saying "no" tactfully is not as scary as it once was.
- *Actual behavior has to match your values.* If one of your team values is accepting failure, then in practice you have to act in a way that supports that stance. It is normal to have a shared sense of disappointment, but the key is not to dwell on this. Instead, regroup and see what you can learn from it and what you can do differently in other projects. This may result in a couple of specific actions such as:
  - There may be some questions you can ask that check, as a project develops, that everyone is still on the same page and you are not being seduced by group logic.
  - There may be more time spent on a particular phase of a project.
  - You may nominate someone to be the constructive challenger in a meeting.

Risk teams – a changing risk appetite

Based on our experience, we would advocate that you cannot really involve your risk team too early in your discussions. Much like the IT team, they will have a lot of work that, when all is going well, no one sees, so they always appreciate notice so that they can plan their workload. Again, these definitely have to be two-way conversations. Below are some topics that we have found it fruitful to explore at a general and project-specific level:

- *What is their appetite to risk, what will keep them awake at night?* This is perhaps the most crucial conversation you can have with your head of risk or risk team as this will shape all your interactions with them. It is helpful to understand their rationale – for example, are they more risk-averse if the context is outside of their expertise, or have they had a previous bad experience? Knowing this in advance lets you frame subsequent requests in a way that can allay their concerns. If some things are an absolute line in the sand then do not repeatedly ask for them (as with the IT team, you want to be considered easy to work with). Crucially, risk appetite is not an absolute but a continuum that changes over time, so this conversation will need to be frequently repeated, especially in the context of research and development projects or emerging technology.

- *What are their processes? Will any of them need to change for innovation?* This is a practically focused chat about how you engage your risk colleagues and what their processes might cover:
  - Who needs to be involved at what type of meeting? What is the determining factor? Is it type of risk, cost, magnitude, or something else? (For example, are you spending £5,000 or £500,000? Are you entering into a three-month pilot or a three-year deal? Are you building something for one client or is this something the whole firm can use?)
  - What forms need completing and when? Where are the templates stored so you know what you are going to be asked?
  - Is document completion a collaborative exercise and are you expected to provide the first draft?
  - What is the approval process?
  - At what intervals are risk issues reviewed on projects – what is the trigger?
- *What is the supplier management process and does this apply to pilots?* Most law firms necessarily have a fairly lengthy and potentially (from the perspective of a supplier) onerous supplier-onboarding process. However, a process that takes many months to navigate is not necessarily aligned with your innovation goals, particularly if you just want to undertake some pilots to see if a particular technology works as described. We are now able to discuss effectively with the risk team and tailor the review process to fit a pilot, whilst still ensuring an acceptable level of risk team review. This can be achieved, for example, because the value of the pilot is low, the documents used in the pilot are all synthetic with no personal data, or we ensure that no data leaves the UK or EU. There is, however, a fine line between enabling access to pilots and knowing enough to ensure that you will not discover any risk red flags that would stop you adopting the technology. It is for this reason that we always insist on reviewing any master agreements rather than just pilot-specific ones, even if just for red flags, then the final version after contractual negotiation as, in the long run, this saves wasted time and effort from the risk team, innovation team, and the supplier.

- *Where are they on the technology change curve?* What they understand about the type of things your team is looking at and what they think of them are useful indicators to help you pitch successfully to your risk team.

Internal client and legal teams – just do it (even if we cannot define "it")

Unfortunately, at some point you are going to have to say no: that something does not work, is not commercially viable, or has lower priority than another. You are going to upset someone. That someone might be emotionally invested in their idea for all sorts of reasons – their client has asked for it, they need something to keep their client, there is an upcoming tender, their promotion prospects are dependent on it, they have promised something to a client without really understanding what is involved, or they have not got what they wanted from one of your other business services functions. No matter how hard this may seem, or how much you may not like a difficult conversation, it is vital to be able to address this early and to quickly develop the skills and thick skin needed to navigate these thorny topics.

We make no apologies for going on about stakeholder management and governance. However, it isn't a one-size-fits-all approach and how you deal with particular people will no doubt evolve as you develop your skills in this area. Your governance process should involve sufficiently senior people who can act as the Supreme Court, i.e. the people to whom upset people appeal. They may not apply their full attention to everything that you are asking them to consider, but it is your job to make their (busy) lives easier by highlighting who is likely to be disgruntled and why, as well as why their request is not being fulfilled, or at least not yet. If your senior stakeholders are forewarned then when their role as Supreme Court comes up, they are forearmed with the answers and can judge appropriately.

Stakeholder management can be a benefit for you beyond conflict resolution; after all, they are intelligent people who can actually help. There is nothing more pleasing than your head of risk commenting that one of your products is exactly the kind of thing we should be investing in, or hearing your managing partner repeat your top innovation party lines to others.

We accept that all of this can seem like hard work and be time-intensive (and indeed it is) but there is a reason that change management consultants say that stakeholder engagement is key to success, because it is – particularly in a people business like law firms. It often feels like upfront time, when time is a precious commodity; but our experience is that it is almost invariably time well spent as, in the long run, it makes your life easier in terms of what you want to achieve.

Chapter checklist

- ☐ Do you know enough about the other teams in your organization that could help you?
- ☐ How can you share information with other departments in your organization?
- ☐ Are you / your team easy to work with?

Chapter 12:
The next big thing – looking forward

It has been interesting writing this book during the start of the generative AI hype cycle as, in many ways, it has made us reflect on why we created innovation roles in a law firm and have since expanded into departments. At the heart of all innovation efforts in a law firm there is a client (be they internal or external) with a problem to solve, and it is important not to lose sight of that.

Has all the digital lipstick gone?[1]

Prior to generative AI arriving on the world stage and its emergence as the preferred solution for the legal industry, it felt like we were beginning to get away from all the innovation theater. We were hearing what people were actually doing and the real problems that they were solving for clients, without hyperbole or caring whether the solution was "AI" or on trend. The focus was on the problem. The focus was on solving it. The trouble with buying into hype and following a trend is that, by their very nature, trends come and go. If you only ever focus on a current trend for the majority of your innovation work, then you become the person who only ever has a hammer so every solution looks like a nail. You quickly become blinkered and lose the skill of ideation and problem solving, which makes it difficult to engage with the next trend. It would appear that the skill with trends is to explore them, consider how you can apply them in your context, but do not get distracted and stop everything else you were doing. Innovation in law firms existed long before the emergence of generative AI and will continue to do so. Keep flexing the innovation muscles of the team by exploring new ideas; keep building and evolving your core skill set – by doing this, you will have the techniques to examine, explore, develop, and reflect, regardless of technology or trend. Remember, "What is the problem you are trying to solve (to which the latest trend might be a solution)?"

Towards a sustainable innovation model

We are used to hearing about sustainability in an ESG sense (which, of course, is an important aspect of innovation but outside the scope of this book). What we mean here is, once you have created innovation out of nothing into something with tangible results and have some success stories under your belt, how can you keep up momentum and enable it to be securely established? We have mentioned on several occasions the need for senior buy in and support, but this has to be more than lip service. Behavior and action has to match rhetoric; it is hard driving innovation in a law firm, and with rhetoric alone you will not be able to put any of your plans into action. We both consider ourselves lucky in that our time at Weightmans has presented us with a land full of opportunities. Yes, you have to take them, but the fact that people who have an idea that they can flesh out are allowed to run with it is something we do not take for granted. The Board and equity partnership backing that trusted us to be able to upskill ourselves and those around us, and to deliver value to our clients and business, has been key to our ability to create what we hope is a sustainable innovation model for years to come.

Innovation strategies are hard. Our first innovation strategy was largely to get through year one and still have a job. We have recently had a three-year strategy agreed by our Board with the corollary investment (genuine support in action) so this is now a multifaceted approach that pulls together strands that cover innovation, R&D, productization, and people (hearts and minds). As we now sell some of our products on a SaaS model, we have created standard license terms and order forms with our risk team, worked out pricing models, and looked at how we bill with our finance colleagues, and put a sales cycle into action (including post-sales account management). The demonstration of real-world value is all part and parcel of sustaining innovation in a law firm.

What next after the O-shaped lawyer? Upskilling future leaders

Innovation is going to remain central to how law firms service their clients' needs and prosper. We know that trends and technology will come and go, but we want to equip our future leaders in innovation so they can avoid the steep learning curve that we had. Training people to be innovative is a task with no end – there are always more people, more trainees, more technology, more problems to solve.

Innovation leaders of the future do not need a deep knowledge of a particular type of technology in order to succeed. In fact, being technology-agnostic is more likely to be useful to them in the longer term. We wanted to ensure that our future leaders have a wide skill set so that they can solve whatever the next set of problems are, using whatever is available at the time. This is what we tried to do with the Weightmans Institute for Future Innovation (WIFI) – a focus on skills rather than technology to be able to solve problems.

Case study: WIFI

Challenge/opportunity

Law firms of the future will excel by recognizing the importance of multidisciplinary thinking, and of providing clients with a wide range of services alongside legal advice. Up-and-coming legal and business services professionals are expected to excel in their legal or technical specialism and must also be able to demonstrate competence in a wider range of skills if they want to enhance their own careers and their value to their employers. It is crucial therefore to embed technology and innovation as business-as-usual at the beginning of careers. The WIFI innovation academy came about from a wish to have an innovation program that covered the approach, processes, and technology that we actually use (rather than "Here is a random way of delivering change from external providers but it isn't one we actually do in practice"). There was nothing off the shelf so we designed it ourselves.

Strategy

In February 2022, we launched WIFI to apprentices, trainees, and junior colleagues throughout our business. WIFI is designed to recognize the growing importance of technology and innovation in the way that we provide services to our clients. It was important to us that any academy provided an overview of the wider technology ecosystem of the firm, so the year-long WIFI program offers insights into technology, project planning, and change leadership, in order to cultivate ground-up innovation and foster a culture of creativity and collaboration.

We tailored the program to equip our delegates with the skills necessary to communicate ideas, work collaboratively, and think innovatively in their roles, in order to truly reflect the changing nature of the legal profession and to futureproof our up-and-coming talent.

People

We hope that it will come as no surprise that people were at the heart of

WIFI! The program was developed having spoken to previous trainee solicitors who had spent six months in the department about the most useful things they had learnt and how they could apply this learning to their future training seats, and ultimately through their professional career.

Execution

There was no existing innovation academy that captured our approach, processes, and technology – so we designed it ourselves. We wanted the content to be contextual and relevant, reflecting what we actually do in practice. WIFI took several months to plan to ensure our delegates got the best experience – one that fitted around their existing workload and reflected our approach to innovation and change.

- *Content.* We split the program into quarterly segments with each topic centered around a core theme, providing delegates with insights into project planning, problem solving, and change leadership. Together, the segments gave delegates a wider insight into the technology ecosystem of the firm and an understanding of the role that they play in fostering a culture of innovation, collaboration, and change.
- *Delivery.* Each quarter included four asynchronous online sessions and two interactive sessions with the aim of:
  - Delivering content in the form of online lectures or presentations;
  - Encouraging interaction between delegates through Miro board activities and breakout sessions; and
  - Providing a space for discussion, networking, and Q&A.

There were four virtual workshop days, where delegates were encouraged to put what they had learned earlier in the course into practice. During these live sessions, delegates were introduced to the stages of planning a project, identified a group project of their own, and worked together to provide a lawtech solution. The groups then had the opportunity to present their finished product and outline the ways in which their technology solution improves and adds value to the current process – ideas included a new starter tool and hub, and a new instruction tool.

Outcome

Attendance and satisfaction have been excellent, proving the new generation's enthusiasm and awareness for technology and the impact it will have on their careers. Over 65 trainees, apprentices, newly qualified solicitors, and colleagues from around the business have joined us. We also used their feedback on topics and event timings to help plan subsequent rounds of WIFI delivery and have successfully started again with a new cohort.

What did we learn?

- *A year-long course is not for the faint hearted.* Running a course of this length requires a lot of commitment from an innovation team. Despite our best intentions to have the majority of the materials prepared well in advance of each quarter, there was still some last-minute delivery prepping. In addition, the actual delivery required a lot of the innovation team to attend to facilitate group sessions.
- *You can teach innovation.* The innovation team has no academic experience in innovation, having learnt everything we know by doing (or at least attempting to do things). However, it is possible to write down how to do innovation and provide people with an environment in which they can put these new-found skills to the test. Getting people together quarterly to work on a project that reinforced their knowledge and skills training was vital to the success of WIFI.

Chapter checklist

- ☐ What methods of training work well in your organization?
- ☐ How can you upskill your colleagues?
- ☐ Is your organization influenced by trends?

References

1 This is a reference to "you cannot put lipstick on a pig" – it was a term that became common in the arena in that a lot of innovation was simply the application of "digital lipstick" to old technology.

About Globe Law and Business

Globe Law and Business was established in 2005. From the very beginning, we set out to create legal books that are sufficiently high level to be of real use to the experienced professional, yet still accessible and easy to navigate. Most of our authors are drawn from Magic Circle and other top commercial firms, both in the United Kingdom and internationally.

Our titles are carefully produced, with the utmost attention paid to editorial, design and production processes. We hope this results in high-quality publications that are easy to read and a pleasure to own.

In 2021, we were very pleased to announce the start of a new chapter for Globe Law and Business following the acquisition of law books under the imprint Ark Publishing. Our law firm management list is now significantly expanded with many well-known and loved Ark Publishing titles.

We are also pleased to announce the launch of our online content platform, Globe Law Online, which allows for easy access across firms. Details of all titles included can be found at www.globelawonline.com. Email glo@globelawandbusiness.com for further details and to arrange a free trial for you or your firm.

We'd very much like to hear from you with your thoughts and ideas for improving what we offer. Please do feel free to email me on sian@globelawandbusiness.com. Happy reading and thank you for your time.

Sian O'Neill
Managing director
Globe Law and Business
www.globelawandbusiness.com

www.ingramcontent.com/pod-product-compliance
Ingram Content Group UK Ltd.
Pitfield, Milton Keynes, MK11 3LW, UK
UKHW021849150926
8657IPUK00005B/162

9 781787 429550